The Chief End of Man

.

The Chief End of Man

AN EXPOSITION

OF THE

FIRST ANSWER OF THE SHORTER CATECHISM

JOHN HALL

Man's chief end is to glorify God, and to enjoy him forever.
Assembly's Catechism

"For of Him, and through Him, and to Him are all things;
To whom be glory for ever. Amen."
Romans 11:36.

SOLID GROUND CHRISTIAN BOOKS
BIRMINGHAM, ALABAMA USA

Solid Ground Christian Books
2090 Columbiana Rd, Suite 2000
Birmingham, AL 35216
205-443-0311
sgcb@charter.net
http://solid-ground-books.com

The Chief End of Man
AN EXPOSITION OF THE FIRST ANSWER OF THE SHORTER CATECHISM

John Hall (1806-1894)

Taken from 1841 edition by Presbyterian Board of Publications, Philadelphia

Solid Ground Classic Reprints

First printing of new edition June 2005

Cover work by Borgo Design, Tuscaloosa, AL
Contact them at nelbrown@comcast.net

*Special thanks to Ric Ergenbright for permission to use
the image on the cover. Visit him at ricergenbright.org*

ISBN: 1-932474-86-2

TABLE OF CONTENTS

Introductory Essay

Is the Shorter Catechism Worthwhile?

Benjamin B. Warfield

The Shorter Catechism is, perhaps, not very easy to learn. And very certainly it will not teach itself. Its framers were less careful to make it easy than to make it good. As one of them, Lazarus Seaman, explained, they sought to set down in it not the knowledge the child has, but the knowledge the child ought to have. And they did not dream that anyone could expect it to teach itself. They committed it rather to faithful men who were zealous teachers of the truth, "to be," as the Scottish General Assembly puts it in the Act approving it, "a Directory for catechizing such as are of a weaker capacity," as they sent out the Larger Catechism "to be a Directory for catechizing such as have made some proficiency in the knowledge of the grounds of religion."

No doubt it requires some effort whether to teach or to learn the Shorter Catechism. It requires some effort whether to teach or to learn the grounds of any department of knowledge. Our children—some of them at least—groan over even the primary arithmetic and find sentence-analysis a burden. Even the conquest of the art of reading has proved such a task that "reading without tears" is deemed an achievement. We think, nevertheless, that the acquisition of arithmetic, grammar and reading is worth the pains it costs the teacher to teach, and the pain it costs the learner to learn them. Do we not think the acquisition of the grounds of religion worth some effort, and even, if need be, some tears?

For, the grounds of religion must be taught and learned as truly as the grounds of anything else. Let us make no mistake here. Religion does not come of itself: it is always a matter of instruction. The emotions of the heart, in which many seem to think religion too exclusively to consist, ever follow the movements of the thought. Passion for service cannot take the place of passion for truth, or safely outrun the acquisition of truth; for it is dreadfully possible to compass sea and land to make one proselyte, and when he is made, to find we have made him only a "son of hell." This is why God establishes and extends his Church by the ordinance of preaching; it is why we have Sunday schools and Bible classes. Nay, this is why God has grounded his Church in revelation. He does not content Himself with sending his Spirit into the world to turn men to Him. He sends his Word into the world as well. Because, it is from knowledge of the truth, and only from the knowledge of the truth, that under the quickening influence of the Spirit true religion can be born. Is it not worth the pains of the teacher to communicate, the pain of the scholar to acquire this knowledge of the truth? How unhappy the expedient to withhold the truth—that truth under the guidance of which the religious nature must function if it is to function aright—that we may save ourselves these pains, our pupils this pain!

An anecdote told of Dwight L. Moody will illustrate the value to the religious life of having been taught these forms of truth. He was staying with a Scottish friend in London, but suppose we let the narrator tell the story. "A young man had come to speak to Mr. Moody about religious things. He was in difficulty about a number of points, among the rest about prayer and natural laws. 'What is prayer?' he said, 'I can't tell what you mean by it!' They were in the hall of a large London house. Before Moody could answer, a child's voice was heard singing on the stairs. It was that of a little girl of nine or ten, the daughter of their host. She came running down the stairs and paused as she saw strangers sitting in the hall. 'Come here, Jenny,' her father said, 'and tell this gentleman "What is prayer."' Jenny did not know what had been going on, but she quite understood that she was now called upon to say her Catechism. So she drew herself up, and folded her hands in front of her, like a good little girl who was going to 'say her questions,' and she said in her clear childish voice: 'Prayer is an offering up of our desires unto God for things agreeable to his will, in the name of Christ, with confession of our sins and thankful acknowledgement of his mercies.' 'Ah! That's the Catechism!' Moody said, 'thank God for that Catechism.'"

How many have had occasion to "thank God for that Catechism!" Did anyone ever know a really devout man who regretted having been taught the Shorter Catechism— even with tears—in his youth? How its forms of sound words come reverberating back into the memory, in moments of trial and suffering, of doubt and temptation, giving direction to religious aspirations, firmness to hesitating thought, guidance to stumbling feet: and adding to our religious meditations an ever-increasing richness and depth. "The older I grow," said Thomas Carlyle in his old age, "and now I stand on the brink of eternity, the more comes back to me the first sentence in the Catechism, which I learned when a child, and the fuller and deeper its meaning becomes:

What is the chief end of man?
To glorify God and to enjoy him forever.

Robert Louis Stevenson, too, had learned this Catechism when a child; and though he wandered far from the faith in which it would guide his feet, he could never escape from its influence, and he never lost his admiration (may we not even say, his reverence) for it. Mrs. Sellars, a shrewd, if kindly, observer, tells us in her delightful

"Recollections" that Stevenson bore with him to his dying day what she calls "the indelible mark of the Shorter Catechism"; and he himself shows how he esteemed it when he set over against one another what he calls the "English" and the "Scottish" Catechisms—the former, as he says, beginning by "tritely inquiring 'What is your name?,'" the latter by "striking at the very roots of life with 'What is the chief end of man?' and answering nobly, if obscurely, 'To glorify God and to enjoy him forever.'"

What is "the indelible mark of the Shorter Catechism"? We have the following bit of personal experience from a general officer of the United States army. He was in a great western city at a time of intense excitement and violent rioting. The streets were over-run daily by a dangerous crowd. One day he observed approaching him a man of singularly combined calmness and firmness of mien, whose very demeanor inspired confidence. So impressed was he with his bearing amid the surrounding uproar that when he had passed he turned to look back at him, only to find that the stranger had done the same. On observing his turning the stranger at once came back to him, and touching his chest with his forefinger, demanded without preface: "Whet is the chief end of man?" On receiving the countersign, "Man's chief end is to glorify God and to enjoy him forever"—"Ah!" said he, "I knew you were a Shorter Catechism boy by your looks!" "Why, that was just what I was thinking of you," was the rejoinder.

It is worth while to be a Shorter Catechism boy. They grow to be men. And better than that, they are exceedingly apt to grow to be men of God. So apt, that we cannot afford to have them miss the chance of it. "Train up a child in the way he should go, and even when he is old he will not depart from it."

Author's Preface

The definitions of the Shorter Catechism of the Westminster Assembly have been always admired for the exactness and conciseness of the terms in which they are expressed. These qualities adapt them to the use of memory, being so brief that they are no burden to the mind, and so comprehensive that they are susceptible of being expanded into a full system of inspired truth. But this very excellence is the source of the greatest disadvantage which has been found in the use of the Catechism in the indoctrination of the young. For the terms of the definitions, though easily retained, are neither so easily committed nor understood as if they were more diffuse and less technical. Hence it is so common to find children averse to the task of committing the answers, and when they have accomplished this, appearing to have very faint ideas of their meaning.

It is believed, however, that this effect is less attributable to the Catechism, than to the mode of teaching it, and that if children were led, from first, to understand the language and perceive connection and comprehensiveness of the definitions, their progress would be both agreeable, and more immediately beneficial. To accomplish this, the use of the Catechism must not be a mere task for the memory, which the catechumen performs by rote,

5

listening to the question only for its catch-word to the answer. Each paragraph may be so explained, illustrated, and applied, that a child can at once attach meaning and authority to the sound, and early learn to discover a mass of practical truth under a short proposition.

Many persons who have learned the Catechism mechanically in their childhood, and under circumstances that connect no very agreeable associations with it, never make much progress in their understanding of it afterwards, nor of the Faith of which it contains the elements, because they have not been taught it as a connected arrangement of sacred truth, but as so many detached and general definitions. In this manner one of the inestimable advantages of the compendium is lost, namely, the permanent acquisition of a system of doctrines in a form and in terms capable of the most important uses to the Christian in the advanced stages of his knowledge and experience.

The author of this work has had in view these facts and these classes of persons composing it. He has selected the first answer in the Catechism as his subject because it presents in itself a topic demanding the first attention of every human being—nothing less than the design of our existence, and the supreme duty of our life. As a secondary object he designed the work as a specimen both to children and their catechists, of the manner in which the Catechism may be made plain, if not attractive, and his aim throughout was to lead its learners of every age to understand, and by the blessing of God, to feel, the personal application of a truth which many of them have regarded in no other light than a sentence for recitation.

Perhaps the volume may be suitable as a text-book for Bible-classes, and some of the classes of Sunday Schools, as well as for more general purposes. It has been with a view to its use in connection with the instruction of children that the illustrations have been more various, and the same ideas repeated in more forms than would otherwise have been necessary. It is difficult to make a strong impression on the memory and understanding of the young, and carry these impressions through a course of reasoning, without much review and repetition.

John Hall

Character of an Evangelical Pastor

John Flavel

"Except you have a knowing people, you are not like to have a gracious people. St. Paul's prudentials lay much in this. 1 Cor. 3:10 'As a wise master-builder, I have laid the foundation.' And indeed this is the master-piece of a master-builder. All your excellent sermons will be dashed to pieces upon the rock of your people's ignorance. You can never pitch upon a better project to promote and secure the success of your labors, than the fruitful way of catechizing.

"What age of Christianity ever produced more lively and steadfast Christians than the first ages? And then the care of this duty most eminently flourished in the churches. Clemens Alexandrinus, Origen, Optatus, Basil, Austin, and Ambrose, *were* all catechists. And it is the opinion, both of Chemnitius and Zanchy, that that exercise which Christ honored with his presence in his youth, was a catechistical exercise.

"We that live in this age have as much obligation as they, and God hath furnished to our hands the best help for it, that ever any age since Christ enjoyed. As chemists extract the spirits of herbs and minerals into some rare elixir, so have our venerable Assembly (lately sitting at Westminster, now in glory,) composed for us the most judicious and compendious system that ever blessed this age. And to make it yet more useful, divers worthy hands have been employed, some in one method and some in another, to make some compendious answers more intelligible to the people. And yet I am of opinion, somewhat may be further done to advance that great design, in a third method, that shall not only make those points more intelligible, than in answering by yea and no; or drawing out the subservient answers to such a length as too much charges the people's memory, but withal to intermix the most useful practical matter with what is doctrinal. If such a course might obtain in all our congregations, I think it would greatly discover our prudence, and turn richly to the account of our people's profit."

1

AN END

When we see a bridge, a telescope, a canal, a railway, or any thing else that man has made, we believe at once that it was made for some particular purpose. In these and the like cases, the things are so familiar to us, that we know the purpose for which they were made; the bridge, to furnish a safe passage over the stream; the telescope, to enable us to see objects too distant for the eye to perceive without aid; the canal or railway, to carry travelers and merchandise from place to place.

And if we should see any thing that had been formed with care, though we should not be able to tell or imagine what it was intended for, yet we should at once conclude that the maker of it designed it for some use. We should not think that any man would expend his time and labor in making articles merely for the sake of making them, and without having some object in view which they were to accomplish.

So when we see a man busily employed at some particular work every day, as a carpenter with his boards, a weaver with his loom, an engraver with his copper-plate, we conclude that each has something that he wishes to accomplish—some one purpose on which his mind is fixed. The carpenter is not sawing and planning and measuring and fitting, merely to destroy his boards and to pass away his time. The weaver is not sitting from morning till night, with his hands and feet in constant motion, for amusement. And the engraver is not sticking the copper only to see how rough he can make it. No: in all these and all such cases in which we see a sensible man so employed, we at once believe, and may almost be said to *know,* that he has some object in view; that something is to be made; and that after a time we shall see that he was all the while engaged in making a table, a carpet, or a picture.

And so natural is this belief to us, that if we should notice even a brute animal employed in some regular labor, we should conclude that it had some design: as when we see a wren busily engaged in collecting twigs; an ostrich digging a hole in the sand by the shore; or a beaver persevering in gnawing at the trunk of a large tree.

Now, in all these examples, the object or design may be called *the end* which the different laborers have in view. The man who with great study and toil invented and then made a telescope, and the little wren who was so active for a day or two in gathering sticks, had each *an end* to accomplish. The end of the one was to be able to see the stars more distinctly: the end of the other was to make a nest. So the end of every machine or work is that purpose which it was designed to effect. The end of a press is to print books; of a mill, to grind; of a pump, to raise water.

It is called the end because when that is accomplished the work is finished—what was wanted is accomplished. The end of a watchmaker, in sitting down to his toil, is to make a watch, and he does not stop till the watch is complete with its works, dial-plate, hands, case, key, and all that is necessary for his purpose. Then the watchmaker's end is accomplished.

Again, the watch has an end. It is to tell the hour and minute correctly. Until it does this it does not fulfill its end. If it moves too fast or too slow, or stops, or breaks, it does not answer the purpose for which it was made, and it must be repaired or altered until every thing is right, and then it answers its end.

And what I have just said of the watch and the watchmaker having both their ends, one as the maker and the other as his workmanship, is true of the other instances that have been mentioned, and of all others of the same kind. Every thing is expected to answer the purpose for which it was designed. And if it does not, and the maker has done his part well, then there must be some fault in the thing itself. The materials have been bad; or something has affected them. Wood that appeared sound may turn out to be rotten; or delicate machinery may have been disordered or ruined by some hard substance getting into it. In such cases the things that are made do not fulfill their end: and yet it may have been no fault of the workman. Still he loses his end.

2

A CHIEF END

When a house is to be built, a number of persons, of different trades, must be employed. The architect makes the plan; the surveyor marks out and measures the ground; the diggers make a place for the foundation, which is then laid by the masons, and upon it the bricklayers build the walls; and after that the carpenters, plasterers, painters, plumbers, glaziers, tin-workers, and other mechanics have each something to do before the house is fit to be occupied. The owner of the house in employing all these workmen may be said to have two ends in view. One is that each man shall do his proper part and no more: that is, that the bricklayer shall do the brick work, the carpenter the wood work, and so on with the rest. His end in employing them is that each may do his part, and just as each does this, is his own end gained. These may be called his subordinate ends. But his great object is to have the house built, and this end is not gained until each workman has finished his share, and the building is complete and fit to dwell in. This end is his *chief end*. He hired a man to dig the cellar; but it was not his chief end to have a cellar, but to have a house. The cellar was an essential thing to be done, but it was only a subordinate end to a chief end.

If you should go into a watch-manufactory, you would find one man making wheels, another making small screws, another little pins, another chains, another springs, and many other men at different kinds of work. In this case, too, they have all two ends in view. Each man has his mind fixed and his hands employed upon his own particular work—the wheel, the spring, or whatever it may be, and the finishing of that work is the end he has in mind. But this is only his subordinate end. The chief end of his work is a watch, and though all shall have completed their tasks, the chief end is not accomplished until the various parts are finished and put together, and are found to fit, and to move the hands properly so as to keep time.

These subordinate ends which have been spoken of, you perceive, are all directly connected with the chief end, and are necessary to it. The house cannot be built, or the watch perfected, unless each of the persons engaged performs his share of the work. But there is another class of ends which are not chief ends, and have nothing to do in producing the chief end, and yet have some connection with it. For instance: a merchant owns a number of vessels, that are constantly employed in sailing to China, India, England, and other parts of the world, taking cotton, flour, and other articles to those countries, and bringing back silks, teas, cloths and various productions in return. The merchant, to carry on this trade, must employ ship-builders, sailors, clerks, agents and many other classes of men. And every time his ship is laden or unladen a great number of laborers are required. All these he has to pay for their services: and in this way he gives support to many families: and it is to obtain this support that the men in his employ work so willingly and industriously.

The chief end of the merchant in this business is to make a support for his own family and to become rich. It is not his chief end to furnish the means of living to those whom he employs. This he must do, and is glad to do. It is, therefore, in this sense, one of the ends of his business; but it has no direct connection with his chief end, as the making of a spring is connected with the making of a watch. If he is a benevolent man it will give him great pleasure to think that by employing and paying so many men he is furnishing the means of feeding, clothing and educating their families, and helping them on to become rich themselves. But though he should starve in poverty, and live in miserable ignorance, yet if his business is well carried on he will gain his chief end.

The Levitical law required the Jewish farmers when they reaped their harvests to leave some of the grain standing in the corners of their fields, and forbade them to glean up the stalks that should fall in gathering in the sheaves. This regulation was made for the sake of the poor, who were by the same law entitled to the gleanings of the fields and vineyards. Now it was one of the ends of the farmer's employment in those days to provide in this way for the poor. But it was not his chief end, and it did not promote his chief end. If he was a kind man he rejoiced in this opportunity of doing good; but this was not the design or end he had in view in sowing his seed, and planting his vines.

From these examples we may conclude that whilst many small or subordinate ends may be answered in the course of any work, there is always one main purpose and design, which may be called THE CHIEF END.

3

THE ENDS OF MAN

We have seen that reason teaches us to expect a design in everything that employs the labor and skill of men, and even of brute animals. The same reason should lead us to conclude that God had a design in all his works. How can an intelligent being look upon the numerous and various things that God has created, and not be convinced that he created them for some purpose? Indeed, this is, as to most of the works of God that we know any thing of, so plain that we are not left to reason about it: we feel, and see, and know, what God's design was. We do not have to *suppose* that the sun, clouds, rivers, and earth, were made for some useful purpose, and not merely for ornament, or to display His power, for we know that we, and all other living creatures, are dependent upon these works for the enjoyment, and the very continuance of our life. In these things the end which the Creator had in view is plain; or at least enough of that end is plain to keep us from wondering why they were created.

Now, can we see the sun giving its light and heat; the rain watering the fields; the streams furnishing drink; the air giving breath; the brutes affording meat, clothing, and the help of their strength to man, and every other work of God accomplishing some purpose, and yet suppose that man himself was not created for some end? Or can we believe that this end was only to eat, drink, sleep, toil, suffer, die, and turn to dust? Either of these suppositions would be far more unreasonable than it would be to imagine that a mechanic would take great pains to make a machine, and provide for its lasting long, and for its being kept in regular movement, and yet have no object in view for the machine to accomplish.

Nor, if it should be said that the duties of friendship, love, and benevolence, are sufficient ends for our race, would this be satisfactory; because how can we account for the creation of mankind from age to age under such circumstances of dependence, without any other design in bringing them into the world than to provide sympathy and assistance for them?

But though reason would teach us to look for design in the creation of man, it could not teach us the whole design of the Creator. He alone can reveal this: and he has revealed it in his holy word, which was written under his own inspiration. By our reason thus enlightened and taught, we are enabled to discover the end of man; that is, the end for which he was created and placed in this world.

From the Scriptures, then, we know that one of the ends for which God made and qualified man was to have dominion over the other living creatures on the earth, to replenish it with inhabitants like himself, and to dress and keep the particular spot in which he was placed. (Gen. 1:26,28; 2:15) Since the first man and woman sinned together, and by their sin caused themselves and all their descendants to fall from their first estate, man has been required to cultivate the ground with great labor, and his toils and sufferings have become great in comparison with the ease and happiness he enjoyed in a state of holy innocence. But he still continues to perform the same ends that he did at first. He cultivates the ground; he keeps the brute animals in subjection; his race is extended over the whole world, and he still remains what may be called the keeper of this earth.

In the case of men and brutes, and the earth itself, we see further illustrations of what has been said about inferior, or subordinate ends, and the chief end. Each muscle, bone, vein, and member that belongs to a living body, whether it be human, or that of a beast, bird, or fish, has its design. But these are subordinate to a higher design, that of enabling the brute to serve the man, and the man to perform the duties that are required of him.

And all the ends of man which have yet been mentioned are of the inferior kind. They relate only to what is accomplished by his body—his strength and his superior power as the keeper of the earth. And yet we have seen that for man the earth itself is but an end. It was made for him. If the ends he fulfils on the earth seem so trifling, when compared with his capacity of mind and the powers of his soul, as to make us feel that they can only be subordinate to some higher and greater purpose of his Creator, then it becomes a natural and most important question, What is the CHIEF END of man?

4

THE CHIEF END OF MAN

This inquiry is one of great interest as a matter of curiosity. For if it is thought to be worthy of the study of the most learned men to discover the nature, properties, and uses of the plants of the earth; its trees, vines, and flowers, and its very stones and soil; if it is considered one of the most exalted and worthy pursuits to learn the construction and ends of the different joints, vessels, and parts of the human frame, surely it is vastly more important for us to ascertain what is the great, the final, the supreme, or chief end of the whole man, considered as a creature of God, and having not only a body, but also an immortal mind, heart, and soul.

But more than this. Such an inquiry it must be our highest *duty* to make. We very well know that we are not like machines that are moved by works, and perform their operations mechanically. We very well know that to labor with our bodies cannot be our chief end, for the only use of this is to keep our bodies in life, and to supply their wants. We know, too, that such labor cannot be fulfilling the final design of our Creator, for it is of no more service to Him, than the feeding of a horse is of service to its master. As in the case of that animal, our labor supplies ourselves with strength and life, but there must be some higher use still which this strength and life are to answer. The power to accomplish a chief end is not the chief end itself. We are bound, then, as rational beings, finding ourselves endowed with such wonderful faculties that answer no direct end, so far as the body and the earth are concerned, to seek for the real purpose of our existence that we may set about fulfilling it.

What, then, is the chief end of man? To obtain an answer to this question, we must know what man is, and what his history is. We have already referred to the facts related in the beginning of the sacred volume, that God created the earth, supplied it with light, water, and food, and then formed man to occupy and use it as his abode. Thus we learn that man is the mere creature of God: that he is the work of His hands; contrived, formed, and provided for by Him: that he not only received life from Him, but was dependent on Him for the means of sustaining it. Man did not make one atom of the earth, of the water, of the firmament, or of the things living or growing in them. They were all made before himself. He was made by the same power as the other works of the six days, and only differed from them in form, until God "breathed into his nostrils the breath of life; and man became a living soul. He was as much the work of God as a tree, or a rock, or a star. He was as entirely in God's power as they were, and could have been used for any purpose that God might have chosen. God might have left his body without life, and filled the earth with lifeless bodies. Or he might have given him only such life as the brutes have; without a mind, or affections, or an immortal soul.

And after God had imparted to man these things that distinguish him so highly above the other creatures, he was still in God's power. His intellect and soul were just as much the creation of God as his head, limbs, and blood. They did not make man independent of God. He could no more continue his life by his own power, than he could have brought life into his body when he was fresh from the dust of the ground. And after the Lord God had made him what he was, and had given him the dominion of the earth and all that was in it, and upon it, man was still subject to God as his superior. God had given him a place to live in, and the means of living. He had not made him a God, and released him from his inferiority. Man had none of the power of God. He could not make a single blade of grass grow, or keep a tree alive, or cause a shower to fall. He had no power over the light or heat, or the wind.

By these various expressions I wish to convey the idea clearly to your mind how absolutely man was, from the beginning, the creature of God; dependent upon Him, and subject to Him. Let this fact be remembered, while we proceed to consider some other facts connected with man's relation to God.

5

OTHER CLAIMS OF GOD

The dominion of God over man, so far as we have now considered it, springs only from his power as the Creator, and from the inferiority and dependence of man. This may be compared to the authority which a father has over his little, helpless child. The father's strength and age, and his relation to the child, on the one hand; and the child's weakness and dependence, on the other, give the father an authority which we naturally admit and acknowledge; and therefore it need not be proved by argument. Such are mankind, though in a far greater degree, in their relation to God. "In him we live, and move, and have our being. He giveth to all life, and breath, and all things. We are his offspring." (Acts 17:28,25) God has thus a natural right over man. He is the Supreme Being; the Maker, Supporter, Preserver, and Ruler, of all. But God's right to the dominion over man is not founded merely on His power and man's weakness. The character of God, and the nature of his dominion over man must be considered, before we see this right in all its extent and authority.

Let us remember, then, that God is a benevolent as well as Almighty Being, and that he designed man's happiness in creating him. He gave him not only every faculty of body, mind, and heart, the exercise of which contributes to happiness, but surrounded him with whatever was necessary to gratify the innocent desires of his nature. We must not forget that life, as it was given to man, was an unmixed blessing. As it came from God it was not attended with pain or sorrow of any kind. Every hour of life would have been full of the most pure and complete peace and enjoyment.

Perhaps you are so much accustomed to connect some degree of weariness or suffering with your idea of life that you can scarcely think of it as being in itself a great blessing. But reflect upon this supposition for a moment. Suppose the choice were presented to you, of having your existence totally destroyed, so that you should die like a brute and be no more, or to be allowed to continue in existence for ever, in a perfectly happy condition, without any possible grief or evil that could occur to make life any thing else than one constant flow of the highest happiness. Would you not decide at once in favor of such a life, and account it a great blessing? Now this was the enjoyment to which man was introduced. He knew not that there was any such feeling as sorrow, or pain, or apprehension. Every thing in him and around him was bright and joyful. God was his father and his friend. He was himself the image of God; he was capable of loving Him; he was admitted to intercourse with Him. Heaven and earth were in friendly communication. God and man loved each other. Man feared no change; he dreaded no sickness. Death was unknown. His prospect was that of endless holiness and joy. God was not only his Sovereign, but his Father; and so good, so lovely, so kind, so bountiful, so holy! It was his happiness to obey the commandments of such a superior, and those commandments were easy, and such as tended to preserve and increase his happiness. Obedience was a new joy; dependence was a delight. He could no more have been happy, or so happy, had God left him to himself without these laws and without this dependence, than the young and loving child could be happy, to be forsaken by his parents.

Was not life, under these circumstances, a blessing? Did not God's power and right as the Creator, and man's dependence on Him, constitute much of this blessing? Can we, indeed, think of it as a blessing, if such had not been the relation of man to God?

Taking into consideration, therefore, the Divine power, wisdom and benevolence, as displayed in the early history of man; and considering, also, the nature in which man was created, the situation in which he was placed, and the kind of government exercised over him, do we not see that he was under the strongest obligations to obey and love God, which can possibly attach and subject one being to another?

Suppose man in this condition to be asked, what is the chief end of your existence? Can you believe he would reply, "my chief end is to enjoy this beautiful part of the earth—to roam about it in search of pleasure, to consider all things as meant only for my use, and to be treated accordingly, to think only myself and my enjoyments from year to year for ever?" Or does it seem more natural that he should say, "I am but a creature. I was but dust, and

God made me what I am. He breathed his own breath into my soul; I am his child. He has given me wisdom and affections. He has made me capable of communing with Him. He is my supporter, benefactor, and counselor. What other end can I know of but HIMSELF? His is all I have and all I am. I am but the reflection of His image. I have no life, nor joy, but in Him. This earth and its productions; this sky and its lights; these creatures, with their various forms and instincts, are but memorials of Him, to remind me, at every look and turn, of the one Supreme source, and to lead my soul to Him. My chief end can be nothing less than to devote myself wholly to my God; to honor, serve, and worship Him; to live to Him, as I live by Him and in Him. And though I have duties to those placed under me and in my care, and duties to my fellow-creatures, whether of my own or inferior kinds, yet these, too, are duties to God, because He has placed me in these relations, and they are part of the means which He has graciously afforded me of showing the honor, subjection and devotion that I owe."

6

THE DIVINE CLAIMS UNCHANGED

I ask the reader if such sentiments as those supposed in the close of the last chapter, do not appear to be those which man would feel in a state of perfect innocence, and in the other circumstances in which he has been described. Are they any thing more than natural and reasonable for a being standing in such relations to his God, and to such a God?

Now it is true there has been a great change in the character of man; he is no longer an innocent being. Notwithstanding these ties and obligations to God, and notwithstanding the wise, benevolent and easy laws by which he was held, he willfully violated these restraints, and by sinning, corrupted his whole nature, and that of his race, for ever.

But remember that this change and fall had no such effect on man's relation to God, as to destroy or affect in any degree his duty to God. God was unchanged. His rights and authority were unchanged. HE was still man's Creator, Ruler, and Benefactor. His goodness and excellence were still the same; unchangeably infinite. HE had done nothing wrong.

HE had not withdrawn any of his blessings from the earth or from man, and thus provoked the sin. Man chose to sin, and having been blessed with the entire freedom of his will, he took his own course and fell. This did not release him from the authority of God: it did not make him independent of his Creator, any more than the disobedience of a child takes him out of the authority of his parents, or the crimes of the thief or murderer remove him from the authority of the country of which he is a citizen.

And the case is just the same in these respects now, as it was on the first day that sin was in the world. God is still the Creator, the Preserver, the fountain of life and of goodness. He is as benevolent this hour as on the sixth day of the earth's history, when He "saw every thing that He had made, and behold it was very good." (Genesis 1:31) His government is just as rightful, his laws as good and as well adapted to make man happy, as they were when Adam was their only subject. Time makes no changes in the Divine nature; it discovers no defects in God's administration; it brings to light no mistake or miscalculation in the original purposes and plans of the Divine mind; it cannot make Him less supreme, or man less dependent.

If, therefore, in the beginning of the existence of our race, it was man's highest duty and happiness to serve and worship God, and live for Him, it is equally his duty now. If he has become "wholly defiled," and by his corruption is "utterly indisposed, disabled, and made opposite to all good, and wholly inclined to all evil," (Confession of Faith, chap. vi. sec. 2 and 4,) it was by his own act that this effect was produced, but this act cannot diminish his responsibility, any more than it can alter the rights of God.

There is a boy who is the object of his mother's strongest love. All is done that a wise affection can do to make him happy, and to endear him to her. The child not only feels that his parent has a natural claim upon his obedience, but he has such a regard for his mother's excellence and loveliness, that the very joy of his young heart is to do her will and promote her happiness. It is his greatest satisfaction to be dutiful and affectionate, and he thinks of no other reward.

Time passes on. Every year only increases the mother's love as she watches and guides the progress of her child. Her control continues to be as judicious as at first; her advice the same as it ever was; her own character equally lovely and her claims upon his regard and duty are multiplied and strengthened by the lapse of years. But during all this time the boy is changing, and at length becomes a disobedient, neglectful, and profligate youth. He has no longer any love for his mother, or regard for her authority; and lives only to shame and grieve her.

But has that mother's claim upon her son been dissolved by his unnatural conduct? Will any one plead on his behalf that his depravity releases him from his obligations? Or will it not be the sentiment of all who know the history, that his conduct is made more base and criminal by the fact that he not only owed the duties of a son to *such a* mother, but that he had himself in his earlier years paid the tribute of his love and obedience to her claims? And does not the loveliness of such a childhood aggravate the deformity of the altered youth?

So it is with man, the child of God. That he has fallen from his innocence, is so far from releasing the claims of his heavenly Father, that it gives a deeper stain to his guilt, and more gloriously honors the law by which he is condemned.

We, then, of this day, are under the same obligations that Adam was under, as the creatures and subjects of God. The chief end of man must be for ever the same; and can that end in this view of the relation be more correctly and comprehensively expressed than by saying it is TO GLORIFY GOD?

7

THE DIVINE CLAIM
IS TOTAL AND UNIVERSAL

We have reached the conclusion that from the very nature of the relation in which God and man stand, part of the chief end for which the latter exists is to glorify his Creator. In what this glorifying consists, and how it is to be accomplished, shall be considered hereafter. It must here he observed, that whilst the divine claim arising out of this relation is universal and endless, there are some facts that vary the heinousness of the guilt of mankind in their neglect of this claim; that is, in their not living for the chief end for which they were created.

1. Though every one by the testimony of Himself and the other works which God has created, and by the light of his own conscience, has a sufficient knowledge of God to bind him to glorify Him as God, (Rom. 1:19-21; 2:14,15; Acts 14:17; 17:27-29) yet the heathen have but an obscure knowledge of their Creator and of their own duty, compared with that which those have who possess the entire Scriptures.

But no degree of ignorance can affect the Divine claim; though where it is not willful, the guilt of the ignorant person is less heinous. A man may have a lawful claim upon me, of which I know nothing. I may be under obligations, which I have forgotten, or which arise, from my responsibility for others, to pay him a certain sum of money. But he has the claim whether I know of it or not. A father may be separated from his child in its infancy and be carried to another part of the world. They may not know of each other for ten or more years, and when they meet neither of them may know that they are related. But this separation has not released the father from his duties to his child, nor the child from his subjection to his parent. The natural rights and duties have not been destroyed; though a violation of them by either, under such circumstances, would certainly not be so sinful as if they knew each other.

2. Although God's claim upon his intelligent creatures is total, there are circumstances which greatly aggravate man's guilt in not fulfilling it.

Some of these have been noticed—such as those which arise from the character of God as a benevolent as well as sovereign Being. The mercies, enjoyments, and deliverances, that men experience day after day, are calculated to draw the affection and win the confidence of the creature, and to increase his desire to please God in all things.

But there is another stage in the history of mankind which brings to view an act of God's goodness that infinitely exceeds all his other mercies, and therefore makes an infinitely stronger appeal to the heart for glorifying Him. I refer to the means which God provided for the salvation of men from the consequences of their fall. Up to the moment in which the probation of mankind was decided by the sin of Adam, man had been connected with God by that bond which is called the Covenant of Works. God's favor, with all its blessed consequences to man, was dependent upon man's faithfulness to the condition of that covenant. That condition was perfect obedience. The moment man sinned, the condition of the covenant was broken, and its penalty was incurred. Man had now no claim upon God. He was a willful, inexcusable transgressor. His sin was the height of ingratitude. God might, not only in strict justice, have left him to suffer the eternal consequences of his transgression, but they might have been inflicted without leaving room for the slightest imputation on the character of God as a benevolent and merciful Father.

But when, instead of giving up our race to these effects of our apostasy, God provided a plan by which men might be delivered from them, be pardoned, and so purified and changed in their nature, that they could be restored to his favor and accounted as if they had never fallen: when in order to accomplish these ends in perfect consistency with his divine justice, truth and holiness, he consented that his own son should be the substitute for the guilty, and should bear the imputation of their guilt and suffer in their place;—when we look at this manifestation of the mercy and love of God, we have an appeal presented to us even more strong than the other evidences of the divine loveliness, to make us feel that it is our chief end to live to his glory. God now appears in the glory of a new character, namely, as a REDEEMER. Whatever conditions or limitations may be connected with the divine purpose in this arrangement, they do not diminish the graciousness of the plan of redemption, or weaken its force as a motive to glorify God. For there are no conditions or limitations in the plan that are inconsistent with the announcement of the incarnate Redeemer Himself.— "For God so loved the world, that he gave his only-begotten Son, that whosoever believeth in him should not perish, but have everlasting life." (John 3:16)

8

THE GLORIFYING OF GOD

The word *glory*, in its common use, means honor, praise, fame. To *glorify* signifies either the procuring of this glory for one, or the act of paying or ascribing it. When a man has constructed any excellent work, such as a beautiful ship, or an ingenious piece of machinery, the work is the means of procuring him honor, because it gives evidence of his skill. The ship and the machinery may, in this sense, be said to bring honor to their constructors. Great inventions have thus secured the fame of men; and the quadrant may be said to set forth the honor of Godfrey; the steamboat that of Fulton; the cotton-gin of Arkwright, and so on.

There is another kind of glory that men receive, which is gained by great learning and talents. As these qualities are usually manifested in their writings, the books of great authors may be said to be their glory; as the poem of "Paradise Lost" shows the genius of Milton; the works of Lord Bacon, Dr. Samuel Johnson, Jonathan Edwards and others, do honor to their writers according to their different degrees and kinds of eminence. This honoring may be also expressed by the term *glorifying*.

Another kind of glory is that *which* a king or other ruler receives when his subjects are obedient and happy, rejoice in his government, and enjoy prosperity. So far as these are the effects of his administration they procure honor to him. Of this description was the glory of Solomon, of whom it is said, he "sat on the throne of the Lord as king instead of David his father, and prospered; and all Israel obeyed him; and all the princes, and the mighty men, all the sons likewise of king David submitted themselves unto Solomon the king. And the Lord magnified Solomon exceedingly in the light of all Israel, and bestowed upon him such royal majesty as had not been on any king before him in Israel." (1 Chron. 29:23-25)

In like manner obedient, dutiful, and affectionate children bring honor to their parents; diligent, regular, and improving pupils to their teacher; apprentices to their master, and so of other relations.

When we speak of God's being glorified, part of the meaning of the word may be explained by these various comparisons. One thing, however, is to be remembered, namely, that as God is infinitely glorious, nothing can really increase his glory; though the different ways in which his power, wisdom, and other attributes are exhibited to man and other intelligent beings, may increase it *in their view.* The sun is as bright when we are asleep or blind, or when it is behind clouds, as at any other time; but we see it to be bright only in proportion to our situation and circumstances. So it is with the glory of God. It always exists in the highest degree: but it is manifested or shown to us in different ways. For instance, "the heavens declare the glory of God." (Psalm 19:1) They do not make Him glorious. He would be equally glorious if there were no heavens. But they *declare* or show his glory, because when men look upon the splendor of the heavenly bodies, the vast space in which they move, their regular motions and their preservation from age to age, they see such proofs of the wisdom and power of God that they are led to admire and praise Him.

This is one of the ways in which *men* glorify God as his creatures. As the mere work of His hands, their bodies and minds show so much of the Divine wisdom, that like His other works, they declare His glory. They do this more powerfully than any other works that God has created, because they are not only material like the sun and the planets, but have life, and faculties of heart and soul, which when they were imparted to them in the beginning of their existence as a race, were all pure. That purity is gone; but still there is enough left in the superiority of man, both as to body and soul, to give evidence of the greatness of the Being who created and endowed him.

So men may glorify God by their submission to his government, and their obedience to all his will. In doing so they give testimony to the Divine wisdom and goodness. Their happiness and submission prove that the plan for governing men was exactly adapted to their case, and designed to make them happy. Every regulation, motive, and restraint, which are seen to operate on man, are shown to have been chosen in infinite wisdom and goodness. All this declares the glory of God. And just in proportion as men approach to complete obedience do they in this manner glorify God.

Another thing to be remembered is that the glory of God is in itself a real excellence. It is not a mere display. When we speak of the glory of a warrior or a monarch, we think of his distinction as arising from the number of his armies, his great battles, extended dominions, wealth, and such things. We do not connect any real good or moral value with such glory. The man himself who has it, may be a tyrant or a monster of depravity. But the glory of God arises from his boundless perfections. It is not an accident, but belongs to his very nature. He is glorious because he is so holy, wise, good, and infinitely perfect. And when we speak of God's making all things for his own glory, we should not think of it as we do when we speak of a man's doing certain actions for *his* glory. In the latter case a man resorts to certain measures to elevate himself into distinction, and to make himself famous, and his motive is selfish and perhaps altogether wicked. But God has no need of any measures to make Himself more glorious; because he is, and always has been, completely so. And he is so far beyond all other beings, that the applause and praise of men and angels can never cause Him to have any feeling like that which a creature has when he is honored by his fellow creatures, who are his equals in nature. This, therefore, is not the object of God in making his glory the great end of all things. But his nature being all that is good, right, and excellent, he is honored by every thing that has that character. And as his laws and purposes tend to bring every thing to this character, every thing tends to his glory, and the accomplishment of it is so connected with the promotion of his glory, that they constitute together his grand design. It follows from this that the glorifying of God consists not so much in any outward act of praise or homage, as in being and doing what God wishes us to be and to do.

And yet it may also be said that even all evil in some way promotes the one grand end of God's glory. For we must not suppose that God can be disappointed in his plans and purposes, or that sin has deranged any of his intentions, or affected his glory. When a family is under the control of the kindest and wisest parents, and their whole conduct and the happy state of the family show that this is truly the character of the parents, if one child becomes disobedient and abusive does this disgrace the parents and their government? Does it not even increase their honor in the minds of their other children and in the view of all who understand the case, by drawing greater attention to that excellence of theirs, as parents, which has been outraged? So, the rebellion and vileness of man only bring into more glorious contrast the excellent government and holy character of God. And if this should be persevered in until the unnatural sinners are sent to everlasting punishment, that very punishment displays and glorifies the justice, truth, and even goodness of the Divine Sovereign.

9

How We May Glorify God

Let us now look at some of the ways in which it is our duty and privilege to glorify God. In order to do this we must consider what means we have of accomplishing such an object: for whatever is capable of being devoted to this purpose, should at once be rendered. As we have received every thing from God, we are under infinite obligations to Him for his favors; and are bound to promote his glory in every way that is possible. Therefore all that we have, both as to our body and mind, or soul, should be consecrated to this as its great and chief end.

To enumerate all these means and methods of glorifying God, would, of course, be impossible. To learn them fully, we must diligently consult the word of God, which as "contained in the Scriptures of the Old and New Testament, is the only rule to direct us how we may glorify and enjoy him."[1] But I will bring before you some heads or classifications which will serve to give a general view of the extent of the

---

[1] Shorter Catechism, Answer 2.

Divine claims upon us, and of the means which he has given us to meet those claims.

1. *We may, and ought to glorify God by doing his will.* The will of God in this connection, signifies all that he wishes us to do, or to avoid doing. It comprehends the commandments which he has revealed to us in his word, and the various duties which are connected with those commandments, though they may not be verbally expressed in them.[2]

The will of God is so holy, good and wise in itself that, whenever it is performed it must show that this is His character: so that God is glorified by any obedience to his will. If a man were constantly to be doing what God has commanded, and avoiding what he has forbidden, his life would honor his Creator by its excellence and happiness. No one could notice his course, and witness the peace and joy which it would produce in the man's heart and life, without acknowledging that such a man was living to his chief end, and that he was following the law of a being who must be glorious, if he had created men and placed them under regulations which could produce such results. This would be glorifying God in the sense of our Savior, when he said to his disciples, "Let your light so shine before men, that they may see your good works and glorify your Father which is in heaven." (Matt. 5:16) He would also glorify God by attributing to Him all the power and disposition to do his will. If a whole nation were living in this way, every person in it doing the will of God in all things and at all times, other nations would see them so happy, so good, so

---

[2] For illustration of this see in the Larger and Shorter Catechisms the answers under each of the Ten Commandments, to the questions, "What is forbidden?" and "What is required?"

peaceful and contented, that if they knew the cause of their superiority above themselves and the rest of the world, they could not help acknowledging that a government was a glorious one that produced such effects: and of course the Divine legislator and governor would be acknowledged as worthy of all the honor of the plan by which these effects were realized. Just as we should, in an infinitely lower degree, ascribe to Solon, Lycurgus, Justinian, or any other lawgiver or ruler, the honor of contriving and adapting the laws to the people, if we found that the laws which they framed and executed, made good, happy, and prosperous citizens in a nation.

There is this difference, among others, to be noticed between the honor referred to in these illustrations and the Divine glory that the obedience of a nation may be secured by the mere authority of the sovereign, or the strictness of the laws. But when God is glorified in the doing of his will by men, it is by their delight in doing it; by their regarding it as their happiness and privilege, rather than a duty which they are compelled to render. We only glorify God aright when we obey Him more as an affectionate child does a father, than as a subject does a king. In the one case it is so much the prompting of love, that obligation and penalty are not thought of. In the other case, men obey because they must. God is not honored by the unwilling service of his creatures. When the heart is not in it, the outward show of honor is regarded as a mere pretence. A multitude of sacrifices, and the most scrupulous observance of Sabbaths and festivals, were rejected when offered by insincere Israelites, as abominable iniquity which the Lord would not endure. (Isaiah 1:11-14)

2. God is glorified by our making his glory the supreme motive of every action. This may seem to be but a different form of expression for the definition of the Catechism which it is our object to illustrate. But my meaning in the present statement is that we should not only regard it to be our duty to promote the glory of God generally by an obedient life, but as far as possible, make this the first matter of consideration in every act of life.

Men are sometimes so devoted to the interests of others that their own interests are absorbed in that devotion. The courtiers of a powerful monarch, especially in some eastern countries, often prove the truth of this remark. Wherever they may be, or however employed in their own private concerns, their conversation, their anxieties, their plans, all show that it is the king, the emperor, the sultan that is uppermost in their minds. For his will or service they forego their own pleasure and interest; deny themselves comfort and ease, and rejoice in their privations and exposures for the sake of the privilege of his service, and the opportunity of showing their loyalty. In our own age we have seen instances of this devotedness in the armies of Bonaparte. In the course of his career he could find at any time multitudes who would readily not only risk, but give up their lives, to show their personal attachment to their leader.[3]

It is possible, then, for men to forget their own interests in their zeal for other men's distinction. And is it unreasonable that men should have such a sense of their duty to God, such views of His infinite perfections, and such a desire to evince their love, as to consult God's glory in every action and purpose?

---

[3] See the instance of this in the Life of David, 1 Chron. 11:15-19.

Now just in proportion as the soldier's attachment to his general, or the subject's to his king, is founded on the excellent character and true greatness of the objects of his regard, does this devotedness reflect honor on their superiors. It is a constant testimony to, and proclamation of the superior virtues and talents of those to whom they give their homage. An army or a nation of such men, would make any man glorious in the sight of the world. In like manner when men live to God, they are real, visible evidences of the excellence of Him to whom they are supremely devoted. And as the Divine perfections are infinite, they justly claim all the consecration of which man is capable—that is of himself totally and for ever; and so minutely, that we may be justly exhorted, in the words of the apostle Paul, "Whether ye eat or drink, or whatsoever ye do, do all to the glory of God." (1 Cor. 10:31) Not that it is possible to connect with the most common and trivial actions, a direct motive in that act to show the glory of God, (though this may be done even in such occupations as eating or drinking, by acknowledging our dependence and obligation,) but this precept directs us to avoid the smallest actions, which are on any account *contrary to* the duty of honoring God, and of so keeping that before us as the supreme aim, that it shall influence our most ordinary conduct. This has been illustrated by comparing our duty to the course a traveler takes in pursuing his journey. A man may leave Boston for New Orleans on business of the most vital importance, and requiring the greatest haste; results may be depending which involve his whole property, or his life itself. His desire is supreme and intense to reach New Orleans. But on his way he may read and converse; he may sleep in the steamboat and in the car; he may eat and drink; yet these occupations are not inconsistent with his supreme aim, and may even be calculated to promote it. They do not retard his progress, or hinder his final object. Still all his conduct, in these unimportant particulars, is modified or influenced in some degree by his predominant desire to reach the end of his journey in the shortest time. So we shall truly glorify God in the smallest details of our common life, if our souls are filled with a desire to honor, serve and enjoy Him. If such is our grand aim and chief end, we shall do nothing in these smaller matters that is inconsistent with it, and in this way we glorify God in all things.

3. *We glorify God by the holiness of our lives.* If our conduct is right, it is because our hearts have been purified and changed: for as the tree is known by its fruit, so the character of a man is determined by his actions. If the heart has been changed it has been by the power of God: and the right and holy actions it leads a man to perform are done through the effect of this power. Whatever excellence or loveliness, then, is seen in such conduct, the praise belongs to the Spirit of God. And this manifests the glory of the divine holiness, just as the heavens declare the glory of his wisdom and power. As none but God can enable a human being to do any thing that is good, so every good action he performs, and every thing he does that shows an holy influence, proclaims at once the praise of God. Therefore the apostle Peter addresses Christians as "a holy nation, a peculiar people, that ye should show forth the praises of Him who hath called you out of darkness into his marvelous light." (1 Peter 2:9.) And so, on the other hand, when those who profess to be under this Divine influence, live unworthily

of the Divine nature, their inconsistent conduct is calculated to lead others to speak evil of a principle which has such bad effects. To such the Apostle Paul said, "The name of God is blasphemed among the Gentiles through you." (Rom. 2:24)

4. *In like manner, God is glorified when the lives of men are usefully spent.* For all men are naturally selfish; disposed to seek their own advantage and happiness, and to leave others to take care of themselves. It is the grace of God that makes them benevolent; and that gives them the capacity and the means of showing their benevolence. God Himself is the highest example of benevolence; it is one of his most glorious attributes. Whatever is kind in any human being, is only a feeble imitation of Him—a dim reflection of His character. But feeble and dim as it is, it points to Him, and should lead men to ask, if benevolence in the mere creature is so lovely, what must it be in the infinite source of all benevolence?

When this benevolence is put into action, that is, when men live to promote the welfare of others, and devote their time and faculties, and improve their opportunities for the doing of good, they manifest this lovely trait, and display, in their humble degree, the glory of that Divine Spirit whose influence has produced it. The lives of Christians, are therefore, said to be "fruitful;" and our Savior said to his disciples, "herein is my Father glorified, that ye bear much fruit; so shall ye be my disciples." (John 15:8) They are expected to be "filled with the fruits of righteousness, which are by Jesus Christ, unto the glory and praise of God," (Phil. 1:11); and are exhorted to let their good example be so evident to their fellow men, "that they may see your good

works, and glorify your Father which is in heaven."
(Matt. 5:16)   It was the evidence of Christ's being "a
righteous man," which led the Gentile centurion at the
crucifixion, to "glorify God." (Luke 23:47)

10

OTHER WAYS OF GLORIFYING GOD

5. *FAITH glorifies God.* The highest honor we can show to a fellow man is to put entire confidence in him. When we believe at once what one says to us, *because* he says it; when we trust our property in his hands, without the least distrust of his integrity; when we have no more doubt of his intending to do what he promises to do, than if it were already done; when we are willing to trust our most important concerns to his prudence and wisdom, and feel perfectly safe in doing so; this confidence shows that we believe him to be a perfectly true, honest and faithful man. This confidence of ours is like a proclamation of our friend's character; it is our open testimony to it. And were a whole community of people to put this confidence in some one of their fellow citizens, that man would be highly honored by all strangers who should become acquainted with the fact.

God is entitled to our entire and constant confidence. His nature is so infinitely holy, that he cannot be otherwise than infinitely true, just, and righteous. Every word that He has spoken or revealed, whether it be history, commandment, doctrine, promise, threat, or prophecy, must be true and must be accomplished. He is so infinitely supreme and powerful, that He must have all the power that is necessary to accomplish whatever He undertakes or engages to do. Those that fully believe these to be His attributes, and confide freely and perfectly in Him in these respects, glorify Him in the sight of their fellow men, by their testimony to His character. This is the evidence of faith. It comprises belief, trust, submission, contentment, every thing that is implied in not merely knowing that God is worthy of entire confidence, but in actually yielding it, and living so constantly in the exercise of it, that it will be seen to be the ruling principle of life. This faith must also include *all* the promises, declarations and arrangements which God has made. It is not enough to believe that He is, and that He is the rewarder of them that diligently seek Him, though this is essential, (Heb. 11:6), but faith is not complete—we cannot be said to have entire confidence in God—unless we believe His testimony as to our own character: His declarations of our absolute need of His grace; and unless we receive, through faith, the means provided in the Lord Jesus Christ for our redemption, justification, and holiness. When we exercise this faith, and commit our whole existence, our souls and bodies, to God through Christ, in entire and eternal submission, we glorify Him in the highest manner of which we are capable in our present state. For we not only testify our highest confidence in thus committing our whole selves, perfectly, unconditionally and for ever, to His disposal, but we show the glory of His grace, justice, wisdom, power, and every other attribute, in the effects produced in us by His Spirit, and in the accomplishment of so great a work by such wonderful means. Just in proportion as we are, like Abraham, "strong in faith," we shall be like him, in "giving glory to God." (Rom. 4:20)

6. *We glorify God by our entire subjection to Him.* He reveals Himself as a King. He takes this name that we may better understand His claim to rule over us as our Supreme Governor, by the very right of His nature and of our relation to Him. We are not bound to Him by the ties of affection and gratitude only; but we are His subjects, and under infinite obligations to serve and obey Him. Nations acknowledge the right of certain persons to govern them. This right has been obtained in various ways, and is exercised in various modes; but the subjects of a king, or sultan, or emperor, bow to his authority, and in some cases submit to his entire control, giving up even their lives at his command. If men willingly submit to such authority, when it is exercised over them by a fellow man, how much more complete should be our submission to one who is by His very nature and perfections over us, and we by our very nature and necessities placed under Him?

And if an earthly monarch is considered glorious in proportion to the extent of his dominions, the number of persons who acknowledge his government, and their willing subjection to his reign, Gen is also glorified by all those who bow to his Supreme kingdom, who delight to do his will, and to speak of his greatness.

There is a special sense in which the Lord Jesus Christ is spoken of as a King. That is, in his relation to believers. He is said to act as a king when he subdues them by his grace, and makes them his willing subjects; when he rules over them by his laws as revealed in the gospel, and by his Spirit in their hearts; when he defends them from their spiritual and temporal enemies, and so restrains, and finally overcomes, all that opposes them, that he brings them to his heavenly kingdom in safety.[4]

Christ is glorified, therefore, by all this evidence of His power, goodness, and grace, as witnessed in His disciples. The more faithfully they follow their king the more He is honored; and, in proportion as He is honored, is the Father glorified.

7. *We may glorify God by ascribing to Him all praise and worship.* Men commonly show their esteem for their eminent fellow men by outward acts of respect and reverence. Subjects bow down before their kings. The Law of Moses required the Jews to rise up before the aged, as a mark of respect. (Leviticus 19:32) We are familiar with such customs among ourselves. On the same principle by which we are led to show this regard to those of our race whom we think entitled to it, we are bound to give the supreme praise and homage to God. There is nothing that commands our respect in man that does not exist in God in an infinitely greater degree. All their eminence is only such as God has given them; it is but the effect of his power. God, as the fountain of this glory, must be unspeakably more glorious, and must be entitled to the whole praise and honor. When men perceive this, and give praise to Him as the Creator, the Benefactor, and the Redeemer, the first and the last, the origin and final cause of all things— this, their praise, glorifies Him. It sounds out His

---

[4] Larger Catechism, Question # 45. Shorter Catechism, Question # 26.

glory, declares it, acknowledges it, and worships Him as the only God.

This is done in various ways. It is offered in the public worship of the Sabbath; in the domestic worship of the family; in the solitary worship of the chamber. It may be offered in the ejaculation of prayer, thanksgiving, and adoration, even in our walks, and in our daily duties. It may be done by our speaking to others of the excellence of the Lord, testifying His faithfulness, and proclaiming His greatness. It is done in our constantly referring all that is good and right to God, as the author of it; and in attributing to His grace whatever is lovely or useful in any of His creatures. In a word, when our hearts are always ready, in view of what God is, and what He has done and promised, to burst out in the hymn of the innumerable host—"Blessing, and honor, and glory, and power, be unto him that sitteth upon the throne, and unto the Lamb, for ever and ever!" (Rev. 5:13).

8. *God is glorified by our spreading the knowledge of Him.* This is one of the most obvious ways of promoting the Divine glory. The man who truly loves God is anxious that the whole world should know of so excellent a Being, and partake of the benefits of this knowledge. The more He is known, the more He will be glorified. We may help to promote this end by bringing our fellow men to read and hear the truth; by showing them the evidences of the reality of what we wish them to see and believe; by entreating and persuading them to consider the obligations they are under to God. And it is so as to our fellow men at a distance. We should desire to see the glory of the Creator, and the benefits of the work of mediation, extended to all the nations of the earth. Whilst men

worship the sun, or brutes, or carved images, they dishonor God. But how glorious would God be were his existence and his attributes to be acknowledged by these idolatrous nations, and his worship to be established! Even man can be instrumental in effecting this change. They may carry or send the sacred Scriptures, and furnish Christian teachers, and thus make God known through the earth. And he who is not contributing all that he can to this great object, is failing in just the proportion of his neglect, to glorify God.

9. *God is glorified by our receiving the blessings of life as from Him, and by our giving Him the praise of all that we, or others, accomplish that is useful or right.* A grateful heart always honors its benefactor; and men cannot acknowledge that every enjoyment they have, and the daily blessings that fall to their lot, come from God, without glorifying Him in the very acknowledgment. And who will not acknowledge it that considers his own helplessness? Who will say that he has power to retain his health, strength, reason, family, friends, property, and the other means of sustaining and enjoying life? Who will say that he can maintain his cheerfulness of mind, and control his evil dispositions, and keep his social and domestic affections pure and happy, by any power that he has in himself? It was decisive evidence of the willful guilt of Belshazzar—"the God in whose hand thy breath is, and whose are all thy ways, thou hast not glorified." (Dan. 5:23)

When a man sees his entire dependence on a Divine Source for these blessings; when he feels that the means he employs, and which seem to be his own, are themselves the gifts of God, and capable of being withdrawn by Him, then he glorifies God by his dependence, his gratitude, his confidence, and his prayers. He joyfully adopts the language of David, "Thine, O Lord, is the greatness, and the power, and the glory, and the victory, and the majesty; for all that is in the heaven and in the earth is Thine; Thine is the kingdom, O Lord, and thou art exalted as head above all. Both riches and honor come of thee, and thou reignest over all; and in thy hand is power and might; and in thy hand it is to make great, and to give strength, unto all. All things come of thee, and of Thine own have we given thee" (1 Chron. 29:11-14).

10. *Joy in God's service glorifies Him.* When religion is seen to be the great source of a man's happiness: when it is evident that he finds its ways to be pleasantness and its paths peace; when his whole life appears to be engrossed with the service of God and the cultivation of communion with Him, what is more glorifying to God than such a proof of His wisdom in suiting the means of happiness to man, of His power in so changing His nature as to make Him capable of such spiritual felicity, and of His mercy in admitting a sinful creature to such privileges? As the general cheerfulness and happiness of created things glorify God as the Creator, so the joy of the heart of those who give their intelligent service and homage to God, glorifies Him as the Father of lights, from whom cometh down ever good and perfect gift (James 1:17).

11

GLORIFYING GOD IN THE SPIRIT

But not to multiply the general heads, I shall comprise under two more the substance of the methods by which we may and ought to glorify God. And these are furnished by the Apostle Paul in these words, "For ye are bought with a price; therefore glorify God in your body, and in your spirit which are God's." (1 Cor. 6:20) The Apostle here states the ground on which this duty is claimed, namely, the obligations Christians are under to God on account of his special right to them as their Redeemer. Having spoken of the infinite nature of this claim, let us look at the two great methods of glorifying God which are here presented, and which comprehend all our capacities. And first, of the most important:

I. *We can glorify God in our spirit.* This expression may be taken to include every faculty that is not bodily. There are the powers of the mind, all capable of being used to the glory of God. Our understanding, memory, and judgment should be employed in searching his truth, in learning what he is, in laying up what we thus learn, and applying it for our guidance. These faculties may also be conescrated to his glory by employing them in making known and explaining these truths to others. The language of one of the inspired writers is applicable here: "As every man hath received the gift, even so minister the same one to another, as good stewards of the manifold grace of God. If any man speak, let him speak as the oracles of God; if any man minister, let him do it as of the ability which God giveth; that God in all things may be glorified through Jesus Christ." (1 Peter 4:10,11)

Every ignorant person that is within our reach is an appeal to us for the use of our faculties in glorifying God in his instruction. And whatever we can do by writing, speaking, or conversing, to illustrate, enforce, and recommend divine truth, and set forth the Divine character, and to proclaim his praise, is a means of exercising our mental faculties in the service of God.

We may also glorify God by our meditations and reflections, which are acts of the mind. These serve to increase our knowledge and love of God; to humble and purify our hearts, and to make us more devoted to Him. For it is through these exercises that the Spirit most commonly imparts his enlightening, sanctifying, and comforting influences. And it is by these that we are brought to know ourselves more perfectly, and to feel our dependence and our obligations.

When our faculties are thus employed we shall discover how wicked and unreasonable it is to regard them with selfish pride, and to use them for our own ambitious purposes. If we have been blessed with intellect and knowledge, we shall see that it was not to lead us to self-conceit, but to afford us the means of greater usefulness in glorifying Him whose gifts they are.

The "spirit" also includes our affections. These are said to belong to the heart, as the other faculties of which we have just spoken, belong to the mind; and we are bound to exercise them in such a manner as will honor God. For example: our love should be sincere and entire towards God, and we should love our fellow-men as ourselves. Such love in itself glorifies God inasmuch as it acknowledges Him to be worthy of our supreme affection, and shows that we reflect his benevolence towards others; and as it also leads us to obey his will with more zeal and delight, and to seek the welfare of our fellow-creatures with sincerity. Hatred to sin in all its forms is another way in which we may glorify God by our affections; for this shows that we admit his views of sin to be right, and have been brought by his grace to see it and regard it as he does. Hope, when exercised towards God and in the subjects of his promises, glorifies Him, because it is grounded on faith; and the confident expectation of the fulfillment of all that he has engaged to bring to pass is a testimony to His glory. And that we may possess this hope is a subject of praise to God; as the apostle, in view of the "lively hope" which Christians are brought to indulge through the resurrection of Christ, exclaims, "blessed be the God and Father of our Lord Jesus Christ" for it. (1 Peter 1:3) And so on the other hand, the fear of God, reverential fear, and fear of his displeasure, is an affection which glorifies Him by its testimony to his holiness, truth, and power; for he would not be feared if he were not known to possess these attributes. In like manner the sorrow, the gratitude, the pity, and other affections of our nature may all be means of glorifying God by their being exercised upon the right objects and from the right motives and principles.

In a word, our "spirit" comprehends the soul as distinguished from the body. Whatever the soul can think, or feel, or do, or cause to be done, may and should be consecrated to the glory of God; and nothing short of this meets the claim of the first and great commandment, as pronounced by our Lord: "Thou shalt love the Lord, thy God, with all thy heart, and with all thy soul, and with all thy mind." (Matt. 22:37)

12

GLORIFYING GOD IN THE BODY

II. *We may glorify God in our bodies.* These, as well as our minds, declare the glory of God, by their exhibition of his wisdom, as their Creator and Preserver. The mere body, whether of men or brutes, considered as a piece of workmanship or machinery, glorifies God by the skill and goodness it displays. But that our bodies may glorify our Creator in the fullest manner, we are under obligation to avoid all abuses and neglects of the body that are calculated to impair its capacity. Every indulgence—such as that of intemperance—which degrades, distorts, or weakens the body, may be said to dishonor the work; just as a beautiful model of some ingenious invention would be dishonored if a malicious or foolish person should defile it, or break some of its machinery, so that it would be seen under great disadvantages. Our bodily health, strength, and vigor honor God, as the contriver, maker, and upholder, of the human frame. But this is a sort of involuntary honor on our part. We are called to glorify Him by devoting our bodies to his service, and to present them, not as burnt-offerings, or in shedding of blood, but as "a living sacrifice, holy, acceptable unto God, which is your reasonable service." (Rom. 12:1)

The body, as well as the mind, is endued with faculties designed for the promotion of the Divine honor: and as the body, as well as the soul, is the subject of the purchase of redemption by Christ, so it belongs to Him. It is called the temple of the Holy Ghost, and is said to belong no longer to the children of God so as to be used only for their own purposes. (1 Cor. 6:19.) To defile or corrupt this temple is a direct sin against the Divine Spirit: (1 Cor. 3:16,17); and the importance of being free from such pollution in our approaches to God, is expressed in the sacred writings by the admonition that in order to "draw near with a true heart, in full assurance of faith," we must not only have "our hearts sprinkled from an evil conscience," but also "our bodies washed with pure water." (Heb. 10:22).

The body is the great organ, or instrument, through which the soul acts; and the character of the soul is determined, in a great measure, by the conduct of the body. All sin comes from the heart, but it is manifested, or affected, by the body. Murder, theft, blasphemy, false witness, and all other crimes "proceed out of the heart;" (Matt. 15:19) but it is the hands that commit the deeds of murder and theft; it is the mouth that utters the blasphemy and false witness. So all that is good comes from the heart; but it must be manifest by the body. Love, faith, benevolence, and other graces, spring from the heart, but they are acted out in deeds of charity, expressions of confidence, and the various other ways by which the feelings are manifested

The faculties of the body are adapted to the soul, and are so many means of helping it to glorify God. The tongue is the instrument of uttering his praises. "Therewith bless we God." (James 3:9) It honors God when it speaks nothing but the truth, and nothing that is inconsistent with the entire truth: when it is pure, and utters no "corrupt communication;" when it is sober, and indulges not in "foolish talking and jesting;" when it is kind, and "offends not in word;" when it is peaceful, and refuses "all bitterness and wrath, and anger, and clamor, and evil speaking, with all malice." (Eph. 4:29; 5:4; James 3:2; Eph. 4:31). But not only by avoiding what is evil is our faculty of speech capable of glorifying God. It is the instrument of conveying "that which is good to the use of edifying, that it may minister grace to the hearers;" it may be employed in the "giving of thanks;" and in "teaching and admonishing one another in psalms and hymns, and spiritual songs." (Eph. 4:29; 5:4; Col. 3:16.) It is the great instrument by which we may exercise persuasion with our fellow men in leading them to the knowledge of the truth, and in declaring what God has done for our own souls. These are but the heads of some of the various classes of methods by which our tongues can glorify God.

The eye may be said to be under the influence of this motive when it is restrained from the view of temptation; when it is not suffered to rest upon that which would provoke covetousness, pride, envy, lust, or any other evil passion. Such self-denial honors the law of God, by the deference it pays to its holiness; and the sacrifice is compared by Christ to plucking out the eye and casting it away. (Matt. 18:9) This member glorifies God when we can say with David, "My eyes are ever toward the Lord;" (Ps. 25:15); and when, "as the eyes of servants look unto the hand of their masters, and as the eyes of a maiden to the hand of her mistress, so our eyes wait upon the Lord our God, until that he have mercy upon us." (Ps. 123:2) So, when the eye is "bountiful;" (Prov. 22:9), and the benevolent man is "eyes to the blind;" (Job 29:15); God is glorified by the good deeds. The eye is the inlet of so many objects calculated to excite the joy, or compassion, or gratitude of the creature; of so many warnings against sin; and of so many opportunities of doing good, that we scarcely estimate as we ought the means it affords us of glorifying God by its proper use.

Similar remarks may be applied to the organ of hearing. It brings to the mind admonitions, instructions, and appeals of duty, each of which is connected with a high and solemn obligation, and which, according as they are regarded, cause the hearer to neglect or improve a fresh means of glorifying God. "The ear trieth words," (Job 34:3): it is one of the channels of understanding, and as one of the subjects of our responsibility we are bound to "take heed how we hear." (Matt. 8:13). It is a channel by which the appeals of our fellow men address our sympathies, or by which we may be tempted to rejoice in crime. Accordingly, whilst the Scriptures pronounce the blessing of him "that stoppeth his ears from hearing of blood," (Isa. 33:15,16), it declares the curse of him that "stoppeth his ears at the cry of the poor," (Prov. 21:13). The ear is also an avenue of temptation, and God is glorified when it is shut against it. It is an avenue through which our hearts may be stirred up to love and duty and to holy joy, and the man is guilty of neglecting the praise of God who does not improve every such opportunity.

The feet are also the servants of the soul, and should be brought into the subjection of the whole body to God. He that ponders the path of his feet, (Prov. 4:26), will see that they do not lead him to walk in the counsel of the ungodly, nor to stand in the way of sinners, (Ps. 1:1). There is seldom a better opportunity offered to the young of honoring God in manifesting their trust in his grace, or a more striking exhibition of the power of that grace, than when they boldly obey this trying precept for escaping from the way of evil men—"Avoid it, pass not by it, turn from it, and pass away," (Prov. 4:14,15). And so it is one of the most decisive marks of a purpose to live for God's glory, when the young prefer the ways of those whose habits and resorts are connected with the Divine worship and service. What errands of benevolence to the souls and bodies of men may not our feet lead us to perform! How much of the character of every day's life and conduct is determined by the circumstances into which our feet lead us!

And we may say of our hands, that they have a share in the instrumentality with which we are blessed for attaining the chief end of our being. What is the nature of our manual occupations? Are they entirely consistent with what is honest, useful, and be-nevolent? How are the avails of the labor of our hands employed? Are we guilty of indolence; or do we go to the other extreme, of devoting our time to gain to the neglect of other duties? Are our hands ever engaged in acts of violence and cruelty? Are they always ready to assist a neighbor and defend the helpless? Do we ever sin in what we write? Do we neglect writing as a means of doing good? Do we consult the Divine glory in the subjects, manner, temper, and motives of what we write?

Should we carry out a self-examination, in these particulars, into their details, we should not think that our hands are an inconsiderable part of those means with which we have been entrusted for the great purpose we are contemplating—the chief end of man.

As pertaining to the body, we might also include in its means of glorifying God, the use of our property, the employment of our time, the exercise of our personal influence, and every other faculty which we possess in ourselves, and by reason of the associations and relations by which we are connected with mankind. For we should not forget that there must be a positive, active glorifying of God in what we do, as well as the mere abstinence from doing wrong. God is not glorified when men live idle, useless lives for every other purpose, but their own advantage. They who realize their duty and their privilege as the sons of God, will joyfully unite in declaring, " none of us liveth to himself, and no man dieth to himself: for whether we live, we live unto the Lord; and whether we die, we die unto the Lord; whether we live, therefore, or die, we are the Lord's: for to this end Christ both died, and rose, and revived, that he might be Lord both of the dead and living." (Rom. 14:7-9.) On the contrary, those who do not understand and seek after God, are characterized by the perversion of every noble faculty of the body: "Their throat is an open sepulcher; with their tongues they have used deceit; the poison of asps is under their lips; whose mouth is full of cursing and bitterness. Their feet are swift to shed blood. Destruction and misery are in their ways, and the way of peace they have not known. They have no fear of God before their eyes." (Rom. 3:11-18)

If we suffer in our bodies for the sake of God, by self-denial, persecution, reproach, martyrdom, or in any other way, we glorify God by the evidence of our faith and our testimony to His truth. It was on this account, that the apostles rejoiced that they were counted worthy to suffer shame for the name of Christ. (Acts 5:41; and see 1 Peter 4:13-16.) When Christ foretold the violent manner in which Peter should be removed from life, he is said to have thus signified "by what death he should glorify God" (John 21:19.) And we find that the patient sufferings of Christians—and it was so even in the case of Christ Himself, (Luke 22:47)—had a great effect in leading others to glorify God.

13

SPECIAL DUTIES

In applying these principles to our own guidance, we should further remember that it is our duty to ascertain what particular ways of glorifying God are open to us individually. We differ from each other in the kind and degree of our capacities, both of spirit and body. Our situations in life also divide us, providentially, into various spheres. These facts are frequently noticed and illustrated in the Scriptures. In the first epistle to the Corinthians, the apostle Paul declares that there are great "diversities of gifts" proceeding from the Holy Spirit. (1 Cor. 12) Among those which he mentions, as distinguishing one Christian from another, are gifts of wisdom, knowledge, language, teaching, governing, helping. He compares this variety of gifts to the different parts of the body, each one of which has its place and function, and is important to the welfare of all the rest, so that no one member can say of itself, "I am not of the body," nor to another, "I have no need of you." And in his epistle to the Romans, employing the same figure, the apostle urges upon each one the duty of attending to the cultivation and use of his proper gift or means of usefulness. "Having then gifts, differing according to the grace that is given to us," whether prophecy, or ministry, or teaching, or exhorting, or giving, or ruling, or benevolence, each should see that he is faithfully using his particular talent and qualification. (Rom. 12:4-8.) And the apostle Peter, expressing the same doctrine, urges everyone to act as becomes "good stewards of the manifold grace of God, that God in all things may be glorified through Jesus Christ." (1 Peter 4:10, 11) In these principles we find the rule of our conduct, and in our Lord's parables of the talents and the pounds, we have further intimation that each one will be called to account for the gift which has been entrusted to him—"every man according to his several ability." (Matt. 25:14-30; Luke 19:12-27). There is no one that has not some ability of this sort: whether of speech, for conversation or preaching; of property, for supporting Christian institutions; of teaching, for instructing the young; of writing, for the benefit of those who read; of ruling, for guiding the affairs of the church; of praying, for the comfort of saints, &c. And the humblest has the ability of a holy example, by word and deed, of doing good to others and of glorifying God. So, again, the situations of persons in life, open to them peculiar opportunities and fields of discharging this duty. A parent has influence in his family, in the circle of his relations, and in his neighborhood. An employer of apprentices and workmen seems called in Providence to exert himself for their spiritual welfare. The magistrate, whether of high or low degree, has a department where his moral influence may be felt. Everyone's profession or business opens ways of access and paths of usefulness, which seem to have been plainly assigned him as the subject of his responsibility. It is our duty to ascertain all these points in relation to ourselves, and to be diligent in the improvement of them, as the special means we have, besides the more common ones, of glorifying God and of fulfilling this part of the chief end of our being.

In attempting this duty, however, we must guard against the separation of our actions into those by which we are to glorify God, and those which do not admit of such a use. We are not truly religious if we act religiously in some things only. The only way by which we shall be enabled to live to God's glory, in the sense in which our duty requires us to do, is by feeling that this is the great object for which we were created, for which we live in this world, and for which we are to live for ever. All our motives, feelings, and actions, as individuals, as parents, children, relatives, neighbors, and friends; as rulers governing, or as citizens governed; as legislators, or as subjects of law; as occupied in our trades, professions, amusements; in short, in every possible situation of life—should have either an immediate tendency to promote, or be perfectly consistent with the promotion of God's glory, as the supreme object of ourselves, of all created intelligences, and of all worlds. We must trace every thing to its connection with God. What is good and right is to be referred to Him as its source: what is wrong and evil to the transgression of his will. We must accustom ourselves to survey this earth, and all that it contains, and all that is connected with it, as one great operation of God's power, beginning with its production out of nothing, going on age after age, in all its changes, down to its final destruction by fire. In this one

THE CHIEF END OF MAN

operation there is a great variety of materials, and a great number of living instruments. The machinery, so to speak, is vast, and in our view complicated, and its parts changing by the removing of some, and the substitution of others. But it is one design, through all the changes of population, and the revolutions of time. It is working on and on to one great point, and that point is the glory of God. What is the END of the whole operation, must be the end of each part. Each material part will do its service faithfully, for it is under the direct control of the Great Supreme Himself. The earth and its seasons, the planets and their revolutions, will not fail in any of their offices. But the intelligent part of this world, being free in their agency; being moral and rational, and not material only, are capable of living and acting without accomplishing their proper end. It is upon these that the motives and obligations of duty must be pressed, in order to affect the performance of their share of the grand design, in the way that is best for themselves, and most glorious to God. And they alone make any approach to the accomplishment of this, who constantly keep before them the one supreme end of the Divine Mind in creating the world, and who look beyond the world's destruction for the fuller development of this purpose in eternity.

The motive of the man who seeks to promote the glory of God, is not only gratitude for the favors which he has himself received, or a regard to his own present and future interest, but he "glorifies him as God;" (Rom. 1:21); acknowledging his supremacy and holiness as in themselves claiming his whole homage. He, of course, pays this tribute to the Divine glory in every form and character in which God manifests Himself; in the mysterious Trinity, and in the persons of Father, Son, and Holy Ghost, and in the different offices of each; Christ as one with the Father, Creator, Mediator, Prophet, Priest, King, Head of the Church, Teacher, Judge: the Holy Ghost, as the Source of regeneration, sanctification, effectual calling, Comforter, Inspirer of the Scriptures. And in each of these persons, offices, attributes, and characters, the glory is not given to one Being separately, or to one distinct attribute only, but always to God, as one perfect indivisible Triune Jehovah.

14

ENJOYING GOD

The Chief End of Man, as we have heretofore considered it, relates mainly to the natural duty and obligation he is under, as a creature, to an infinitely great, good, and holy Creator. In this relation he is bound to seek the glory of God, as the supreme motive of his life. But the design of God did not end here. He did not create man to exhibit His power and wisdom, as is done by the volcano, the ocean, the firmament, and His other works, without connecting with this purpose a design to make the very performance of his duty the means of blessing man. He so formed human nature, as to unite man's greatest happiness with his natural duty: so that to be supremely blessed, it was only necessary that man should be perfectly faithful. The happiness of man was, therefore, one of the objects of God in creating him: and He made this object concurrent with the other. And the happiness which He designed should accompany and proceed from his glorifying Him, was not of an inferior grade; not such as the brutes have, though they are happy. It was to be a happiness of the most exalted kind, as well as endless in its duration. Now of what should such happiness consist? It must be derived from objects of the highest perfection. Nothing imperfect; nothing that is capable of being exhausted; nothing that is limited by time; nothing that is not fuller and greater than the resources of man in himself, can answer this purpose. The least deficiency in any of these qualities would make the proposed means of happiness insufficient. It requires but little reflection to determine that nothing in the universe can come up to this demand, but the attributes of God Himself. There is no created object, or combination of objects, that are great enough, or enduring enough, to equal the capacity of the eternal human soul. For remember that it was, originally, made in the likeness of God's nature; that, however inferior in extent, the faculties of the human soul have a resemblance to those of the Divine nature; so much so, that man was capable of a degree of fellowship with his Maker. And, though this fellowship was lost by our fall in Adam, it is capable of restoration and of ultimate perfection through Christ. So that it may be still said of our nature, that it is susceptible of that fellowship. To become like God; to be capable of loving Him and of receiving His affection; to hold spiritual intercourse with Him; to obtain from Him perpetual communications of His grace, love, wisdom, and all spiritual advancement and glory; to be elevated, as it were, from the rank of subjects or creatures, to the place of children; and to have this relation made perpetual, without abatement or reverse for ever; this must be the highest happiness of which our nature is capable: it must perfectly fill our desires. If there is one term by which this condition of felicity can be expressed, I know of none more concise and comprehensive than that of ENJOYING GOD.

This, therefore, must be considered as part of the end for which man was created, and as part of the end which man is to keep before him throughout his life. It is connected with the glorifying of God, in the proposition before us, as our duty and its reward are constantly united, and because this reward is so combined with the duty in the very nature of both, as to be like one object in the mind of the person who is following the chief end of his nature. He who seeks, from right motives, (and of course under the influence of the Holy Spirit,) to glorify God in all that he does, has such an appreciation of the excellence of God, loves it so supremely, and is so far conformed to it in the leading characteristics of his renewed nature, that God Himself becomes the portion that his soul desires, and he can fix his mind on nothing less than God, that is satisfactory. Every act in which he engages with this view, is not as a mere tribute to God—a momentary or even a constant homage—but is so combined with love, and with the aspirations of his heart after God, as the object of his supreme affection and desire, that it is also an effort to associate the soul more closely with God: as a son, who is devotedly attached to his father, finds in every act of reverence, in every sentiment of esteem, and in every word of applause in which he indulges, in reference to his parent, a fresh tie; it is an expression of attachment which tends to warm and strengthen the attachment.

15

EXAMPLES AND ILLUSTRATIONS

To understand this idea more definitely than descriptive language can present it, let us refer to some of the impassioned expressions in the Psalms, as those of a heart that is living to the glory of God as its chief end, and we shall see how intense becomes the aspiration after the enjoyment of God. Such as, (Psalm 84:2) "My heart and my flesh crieth out for the living God." (Psalm 42:1,2) "As the hart panteth after the water brooks, so panteth my soul after thee, O God. My soul thirsteth for God, for the living God: when shall I come and appear before God?" (Ps. 73:25,26) "Whom have I in heaven but thee? and there is none upon earth that I desire besides thee. My flesh and my heart faileth; but God is the strength of my heart, and my portion for ever." (Psalm 63:1) "Oh, God, thou art my God! early will I seek thee: my soul thirsteth for thee, my flesh longeth for thee in a dry and thirsty land where no water is." Such exclamations as these are not simply hymns of praise and adoration, or petitions for transient blessings, or for large measures of grace. They are the language of a soul that DESIRED GOD, and that looked beyond the restraints of time, the body, and the earth, and expected full satisfaction only in heaven. Illustrations to the same effect might be quoted from the epistles of the New Testament, from the description of the New Jerusalem in the Apocalypse, and from Christian biography.

The enjoyment of God, then, is the chief end of man, under two aspects. It was the design of God that man's complete happiness should be found in the Divine favor; and that this happiness should be the result of man's living to his Creator's glory. It is also man's chief end or design, in his own mind; because when he devotes himself to God he pursues the enjoyment of God as the only blessing that can satisfy the holy affection that has been awakened by the operation of the Spirit on his heart. And, this he does not pursue as an enjoyment only, but as the highest means and opportunity of developing and expanding the holy exercises of his soul.

Let us employ again such feeble illustrations as our earthly experience can furnish, in order to understand more clearly the nature of this enjoyment. What is it in friendship that at the same time gives it its greatest strength and its highest gratification? Say that the friendship of two individuals is founded on the highest esteem for each other's virtues, mutual admiration of character, and general sympathy of disposition and taste. Thus united, and cherishing the tenderest emotion towards each other of which the heart is capable, what is it that produces, feeds, and gratifies those emotions? Can you separate the causes from the effects? the emotions from the individuals?

Can you imagine of two friends, A and B, that A loves every quality of B, but does not love B himself; and that the same is true of B in reference to A? Is it pure, absorbing friendship if the two, respectively, are just as content to be separated as together; just as willing to live at opposite sides of the earth as in the same neighborhood; and satisfied to pass through life without communication, correspondence, or intercourse? Apply the same inquiries to the domestic relations of brothers and sisters, parents and children. Does not nature exert all her force in drawing their hearts together, in making them impatient under separation, and in clustering them all in one group if they are to be perfectly happy in these relations?

And does not this enjoyment of each other, this heartfelt affection, this communion strengthen and deepen the friendship and the love in these several cases? Does not the child, or the sister, or the friend find the attraction of their hearts to the parent, the brother, or the friend, stronger when they are in habits of daily intercourse than when their interviews are broken by long intervals?

And do they not all find that the means of strengthening the bonds of their union are the means of increasing their happiness in each other?

And yet no one of them would say that all he regards the other for is as a means of making himself happy. The affection of parents and children is not a selfish emotion: nor is that the case with any species of pure friendship. Their enjoyment of each other is the result of the affection already existing. It was not the first motive; but the natural result, and the chief element of this enjoyment is that it is the fuller expansion of the affection: it is the manifestation and action of what was less enjoyed, because though it existed, it lay comparatively dormant for want of exercise.

So when we speak of enjoying God, we mean to include that state of heart towards Him which seeks His presence and Himself, as the appropriate gratification of our affections, and not as an end separate from such a state. It is therefore connected with glorifying Him as a part of the chief end of our being, as both are the effects of a principle which causes man to acknowledge and desire God as the chief good.

16

HOW GOD IS ENJOYED

But in what ways can creatures so inferior as we are be capable of enjoying the infinite and supreme God? I answer,

1. We enjoy God through the influences of the Spirit which we receive. By these God manifests Himself to the hearts of his renewed children, and forms the chain of communication which connects them with heaven. Most of these influences are the means of direct happiness, and those which are disciplinary lead to happiness eventually by purifying and correcting the soul. There, for instance, is the peace which flows from a sense of pardon and reconciliation, and which is described as passing all understanding, (Phil. 4:7). And there is also the peace which attends the perfect repose of the soul in God through faith, and which is the subject of the prophet's assurance—"Thou wilt keep him in perfect peace whose mind is stayed on thee, because he trusteth in thee," (Isaiah 26:3). That trust or faith is a fruit of the Spirit, and is the source of the highest enjoyment of God; removing fear, and being the exercise of that fond, affectionate reliance which is

the sweetest ingredient of earthly friendship, and which acts with infinitely greater power when its object is God Himself. When God thus by his sweet encouragement and gracious drawing, brings the soul to exercise undivided, loving confidence in Himself, it is a means of enjoying Him. It brings Him nigh; evidences what is hoped for; realizes what is unseen; gives a token of his love and a proof of his nearness by the strength which it imparts and the contentment it inspires. With such peace, love, and faith, there must be joy. Each alone is joy: and the joy is in proportion to their degree. Gentleness, goodness, meekness, longsuffering, and temperance, which are also among the fruits of the Spirit, (Gal. 5:22,23), are all blessed in their effects upon the heart, directly; indirectly promote its purest happiness, and are so many breathings of the Divine nature itself. He who partakes of them knows that they are from Him who is the highest object of his love, and each influence is a remembrance of that Divine affection by which his heart was first taught to love his God. (1 John 4:19.)

2. God is enjoyed by our communion with Him. The spiritual graces of which we have just spoken tend to keep the soul in intercourse with their source; but the heart is often drawn into peculiar abstractions from the world, and brought as it were into spiritual conversation with God. Not in visions, or trances, or illusions, created by excitement and fanaticism; but in humble, child-like, docile waiting upon God; meditating on his perfections; contemplating his works of love and mercy; surveying his ways of providence, redemption, and grace, whilst God Himself seems to be passing them before the mind, interpreting them, impressing them, exhibiting their meaning, and throwing around them the charms of his

love. Such seasons may not improperly be called interviews with God; He is felt to be very near and very precious. The solitary musings of one, as he brings to mind the voice, and the countenance, of a deceased friend, and the tender incidents of intercourse that death long since dissolved, often seem to bring back the scenes of departed years with the vividness of the events of yesterday. But in communion with God, the friend lives: he is near us, and with us, and speaks to our hearts, and as it were breathes upon us the influence of his spirit.

3. The means of grace are opportunities of enjoying God. Through his *word* we learn His character and His will. It is the portrait of Himself, in which His most glorious and lovely attributes are drawn; and the contemplation of it is a source of direct enjoyment to him who delights in His image. This viewing of God in His written word, not only gratifies the affectionate longings of the heart towards Him, but tends to assimilate the beholder to the object. For, as in all other modes of communion with God, the soul laying itself open to the entire influence of the great object of its attachment, will be molded and changed and conformed more and more into a resemblance to the character that is so much esteemed. Here the words of the apostle may be applied—"We all, with open face beholding as in a glass the glory of the Lord, are changed into the same image from glory to glory, even as by the Spirit of the Lord" (2 Cor. 3:18). And the revealed word being also an expression of what the Divine will is as to the conduct of men, and of what is pleasing to God, the child of God finds that it opens to him a new means of enjoyment by obedience. His language is—"I

delight to do thy will, O my God; yea, thy law is within my heart." "My soul breaketh for the longing that it hath unto thy judgments at all times." (Ps. 40:8; 119:20) This obedience, again, helps to bring him more into the likeness of God, and into greater capacity and desire to enjoy Him. Here, too, the soul finds those expressions of tender affection, and the record of those deeds of affection, which he cannot peruse without having his emotions enkindled into fresh warmth. *Prayer* is another means of access to the fountain of enjoyment. Is conversation one of the most efficient methods of strengthening attachment between mortals? so is the influence of communion with God by prayer. Prayer is not only the offering of petitions, the expression of confidence, the act of devotion—but it is the opening of the whole heart to God in child-like confidence: the speaking out of its feelings, as well as its desires. Thus prayer is not only blessed in procuring deliverance from evil, and the bestowment of good, but the very admittance to the privilege of God's presence is joy. I may here refer again to the book of Psalms, for the best actual examples of prayer as the channel of enjoying God. How expressive are the terms in which David declares the effect of his prayers! "O taste and see that the Lord is good." "Come and hear all ye that fear God, and I will declare what he hath done for my soul." (Ps. 34:8; 66:16). The *sacraments* are blessings of the same kind. How near does the believer stand to God, and how tenderly does God stand by him as his Father, when baptism devotes his children to Him! How does the condescension of Divine love seem to stoop to take up his abode under our very roof when the Christian family sit together at the Lord's Table and share the emblems of his enduring love! What a combination of means is presented in this single ordinance to evince every demonstration of Divine affection, and to awaken it in the heart of the partaker! Its form—that of a social meal; its food—the representation of his highest act of love; its company—his friends and ours; its authority—his own appointment; its blessing—his own spiritual presence; its past memorial—that of what he did for us; its future memorial—that of what he is to do at his coming. Who can be admitted to such a privilege and not joy in God through our Lord Jesus Christ, by whom we have now received the atonement?" (Rom. 5:11).

4. To these heads might be added many others specifying the means of enjoying God, and illustrating the nature of that enjoyment. Every thing, in fact, ministers to this end in the heart of the adopted child of God. When he surveys the outward works of creation; and the course of God's providence, he is reminded of the object of his affections and regards them as so many tokens of his excellence. Whilst he is endeavoring to glorify Him in a life conformed to his will, he finds it a source of divine enjoyment. His daily duties, benevolence and zeal are blessed to the same end, for in them all he lives as to the Lord and not to man only. This supreme aim consecrates all he does; and whatever connects him with God, connects him with the enjoyment of Him as the portion of his soul.

17

ENJOYING GOD FOREVER

These are no more than some fragments of the beginning of the saint's enjoyment of God. They relate only to the glimpses of God which he obtains in this life, and to means of enjoying Him, which are subject to interruption, to the influence of mortal frailty, to the obscurities, weaknesses, and corruption of the bodily state. We may enjoy God for ever. And to form any conception of the increase of this enjoyment above that which is possessed in this world we must bear in mind several particulars of the different circumstances in which men will be placed.

1. They will then be entirely spiritual and there will be none of those clogs of sense which so seriously interrupt the continuance of spiritual joy here, and which keep it so low in its degree. The wants and infirmities of the body in this life are so many weights and impediments to the soul, and he whose heart is set upon glorifying and enjoying God will be constantly prompted to exclaim "who shall deliver me from the body of this death!" (Rom. 7:24)

2. They will be entirely holy. Nothing cements the union and affection of hearts so much as

similarity of character. So long as any sinfulness remains in the heart, the enjoyment of a perfectly holy God must be far below what it is when by the complete removal of sin, and a final abandonment of a sinful state, there is an assimilation of the human spirit to that of the divine. Death removes this last impediment, and the soul finds the intensity of its love and desire for God and the capacity for such enjoyment to be immeasurably advanced, when from its prison of corruption, dishonor, and weakness in the natural body, it is raised to the incorruption, glory, and power of the spiritual body. (1 Cor. 15:43,44.) "It doth not yet appear what we shall be; but we know that when he shall appear we shall be like him, for we shall see him as he is." (1 John 3:2).

3. In heaven the saints will enjoy far more intimate and clear perceptions of the glory of God. Their views of God in the flesh are at the best obscure and distant, compared with what they desire. But this they must endure so long as they remain in a world which is still under a curse, and where the divine glory is only manifested to a few. In heaven, this glory is the very light of the place. (Rev. 21:23) No longer an occasional and short gleam, as it shines on the soul in its earthly tabernacle, it is now its atmosphere perpetually, and "the nations of them that are saved shall walk in the light of it." (Rev. 21:24). Means, symbols, channels of communing with God and knowing Him will be no more needed. "The Lord God Almighty and the Lamb are the temple." (Rev. 21:22.) Access will be direct, open, constant, "and they shall see his face." (Rev. 22:4).

4. Their enjoyment will be further enhanced by the expansion of their own powers; the growth of their knowledge; their increasing understanding of the

divine character, of God's works and operations. All this constant enlargement and elevation will be identifying them more and more with Heaven and with God. Their enjoyment will so increase that no source of joy can be imagined that is disconnected from God Himself. And,

5. To crown the perfection of the enjoyment it will be eternal. How it impairs the enjoyment of friendship here to know that it is soon to be interrupted by separation, and that the affection on one side or the other, or both, may be chilled or diverted by the lapse of time! But no time can affect the union of God and the soul. Separation is impossible. The joy will be full and it will endure for ever. As the perfections of the Divine Being are infinite, they can never be exhausted as sources of blessedness and felicity to the redeemed. They cannot satiate by their excess. There will be an eternal progress of the soul in its own gloriousness and in its satisfaction with God.

It must be evident that the tendency of keeping such enjoyment as this before the mind as a Chief End, is to promote holiness, likeness to God, and conformity to his will. And where these results are attained there must be corresponding happiness, which is in substance the enjoyment of God.

18

PREPARATION TO ENJOY GOD

It is clear that there are certain requisites for the enjoyment of God as it has been described. Man, in his fallen state, would not find God an object of desire. He would not naturally seek communion and fellowship with Him, and to live in the glory of his presence for ever, as the means of his greatest happiness. He must, therefore, know God; must be able in some degree to understand and appreciate his loveliness; must esteem and love Him; must have his own nature brought into such a degree of similarity to the divine, as to admit of congeniality; must have a strong sense of his entire dependence on God, not only on his providence as the Creator, but on his grace and mercy in the relation of God, Redeemer, and Sanctifier. He must also have a humble sense not only of his natural inferiority and of the still wider separation between God and him by reason of sin, but of that elevation to which he is raised in being called the child of God: regarding it not as bringing him to an equality with God, or giving the least occasion for complacency or presumption, but as an act of infinite condescension and grace, the greatness of which will never be diminished in eternity.

When the soul has been released from its fetters and encumbrances on earth, and attains the free and unclouded bliss of heaven, it will find that the enjoyment of God has been throughout all its existence connected with the glorifying of God: and that this will be its Chief End in heaven, as it was on earth; for eternity, as well as in time. To speak of his glory, to manifest it, and to adore it will be for ever incorporated with the service of God. To view it and partake of it will be an element of the happiness of heaven, and will be more literally than it has been on earth, the enjoying of God. This glory emanating from the blessed Savior will be communicated to his people, and be made their everlasting inheritance. "The glory which thou gavest me, I have given them. Father, I will that they also whom thou hast given me be with me where I am; that they may behold my glory which thou hast given me." (John 17:22,24).

The Son of God, who uttered these words, was, whilst on the earth, both a manifestation of what the Divine glory is, and an example in our own nature of what constitutes man's living to his chief end. Men "beheld his glory, the glory as of the only begotten of the Father" (John 1:14); and it was a real, sometimes an overpowering glory. But it did not consist in any of the outward incidents by which men acquire glory. Utterly destitute of these—and by assuming the very form of a servant showing his entire independence of them—there was a glory in his character which made a more awful impression on those who discerned it, than the Divine power which was exhibited in his miracles. It was his perfect holiness, his uniform goodness, his Divine loveliness, his unchanging, unwavering, and complete rectitude, under all circumstances, in all relations, and at all times, that manifested Him to be more than human, as much as his raising of the dead, or controlling of the wind: and that invested Him with as true a glory in the streets of Capernaum, or on the shore of Gennesaret, as when the voice of the Father, the descent of the Spirit, and the opening of the heavens designated Him at his baptism; or when in the holy mount of transfiguration in the hearing of those who were "eye-witnesses of his majesty" He "received from God the Father honor and glory." (Matt. 3:16,17; 2 Peter 1:16-18).

So the glory of God is accompanied with infinite power and greatness; but that is not the only ground on which our worship and service are claimed. God, as He is in Himself and for Himself, is supremely entitled to our affections and to ourselves. As we cannot in our present life rise to the full contemplation or understanding of such boundless attributes and excellence, we may dwell upon them in that veiled form in which they are manifested in the life of Christ on earth. And he who faithfully observes the character of Christ in his words, actions, and spirit, will have as strong a reflection of the supreme perfections as his sight can bear.

As an example of living to the chief end of man, the life of Christ is equally perfect. Particular references on this point, or on the other one just mentioned, would fail to give any adequate impression of its fullness in this respect. Let the reader be persuaded to give the four gospels at least one deliberate perusal with this single view; namely, to trace the life of Christ in its manifestations of the Divine glory, and in its consecration to God. If the reader will not take this slight means of pursuing this great subject, let him not refuse at least such a perusal of the gospel by John. Let him carefully notice the expressions, the conduct, the spirit, the miracles, the prayers, the sufferings of the blessed Savior, and see how the glory of God is visible in them as the motive and the reward of every one: how it excluded selfishness; made worldliness contemptible, and kept spiritual things in a prominence which was never obscured by things temporal.

Such an examination will also show that in all respects in which the human nature of Christ during his humiliation can be regarded separately from the Divine, the Savior manifested how the eternal enjoyment of God may be kept in view as part of man's chief end. His whole course had this direction. His prayers, retirements, and conversations show that he resorted to God for such comfort and joy as he allowed Himself to partake of in his state of incarnation: and as he draws near the end of his mission, he speaks not of the glory and power he was immediately to resume, so much as of his identity with the Father, and of his returning to the Father. This is very observable in the comforting address to his disciples, and in the prayer which follows it in the gospel by John 14-17. To return to the Father, to partake of his glory, and to glorify Him, and thus to enjoy Him for ever, are the pervading sentiments of that delightful passage. "Glorify thy Son, that thy Son also may glorify thee. Glorify thou me with thine own self. And now I come to thee. I in them, and thou in me, that they may be made perfect in one" (John 17:1, 5,13,23). And the Spirit, through Paul, in like manner represents this returning of Christ and the final closing of his Mediatorial work as accomplishing the universal felicity of heaven by so bringing all things into harmonious subordination "that God may be all in all." (1 Cor. 15:28).

19

APPLICATION OF THE WHOLE

Reader! The inquiry, in which we have been engaged, is not one of mere theological speculation. Its object has not been only to expound and illustrate a concise proposition. The design of choosing it as a subject of exposition was to lead your mind to the practical conviction that you are under infinite obligation— both as it regards your duty and your eternal happiness—to make the glory of God and the full and everlasting enjoyment of Him the first, supreme, and eternal motive of your whole life.

Has the claim been established? Is it unreasonable? Is it not just, necessary, and even infinitely good? How, then, does your life stand in relation to this claim? Perhaps, by your outward connection with Christ in the Church, you profess to be a servant of God, redeemed by the blood of Christ, and are thus under an accumulated obligation to glorify God in your body and spirit, which are God's. But is this truly and plainly the chief end of your pursuit? Is it your engrossing object? Are all others subordinate and subsidiary? Review the pages you have just perused, with the personal application of these questions to your life and conscience, and judge these questions to your life and conscience, and judge whether you are fulfilling the chief end of your creation and redemption.

If the reader is one who makes no such profession, let me say to him before he dismisses the subject, are you not convinced that the glory of God and the eternal enjoyment of Him are the objects which you are bound to pursue, as the creature of God and the subject of his boundless goodness? Are you not convinced that nothing less than the glory of God is worthy of the supreme aim of the immortal faculties which he has given you, and that nothing less than Himself can satisfy the immortal capacity of these faculties? Are you content to live in the possession of such powers, and in the enjoyment of such mercies, and yet be wholly unfaithful to the very first object of your existence and the primary design of your endowments? Will you continue to make yourself the termination of your aims? Will you set up your own honor, distinction, wealth, and enjoyment in rivalry of, and to the total exclusion of the glory of THE KING ETERNAL, IMMORTAL, INVISIBLE, THE ONLY WISE GOD? (1 Tim. 1:17). Yet is not this the tendency of your life, if it be not wholly devoted to God? And do not the reflections of this volume commend themselves to your reason in establishing the truth that in thus substituting yourself for God, you mistake the true means of securing happiness? Compare yourself—rational and immortal— with the pursuits that engage your chief regard. Whatever may be their merit in other respects, however dignified and agreeable, let me beg you to consider whether they must not inevitably fail to suit your wants if they are not as immortal as yourself? That mind of yours, so craving in its desires for knowledge and understanding; those affections, so restlessly bent upon seeking an object for their complete gratification, are to survive the body which they now inhabit. Their powers will not be changed: their capacities not diminished; their desires will not die. Will your present means of gratification survive with them? Are they spiritual? Are they holy? If they are neither, they cannot pass with you into a spiritual world, or if they did, they could not make you happy there. Be wise. Be humble. And if you have been living thus far to the flesh, seek even now the power of that Divine grace which can renew your nature, reconcile you to God, and enable you to glorify and enjoy Him both now and for ever. "For of Him, and through Him, and to Him are all things; to whom be glory for ever. Amen" (Rom. 11:36).

THE END

Other Solid Ground Titles

In addition to the book *The Chief End of Man* which you hold in your hand, Solid Ground is honored to offer many other uncovered treasure, many for the first time in more than a century:

THE COMMUNICANT'S COMPANION by Matthew Henry
THE CHILD AT HOME by John S.C. Abbott
THE LIFE OF JESUS CHRIST FOR THE YOUNG by Richard Newton
THE KING'S HIGHWAY: *The 10 Commandments for the Young* by Richard Newton
HEROES OF THE REFORMATION by Richard Newton
FEED MY LAMBS: *Lectures to Children on Vital Subjects* by John Todd
LET THE CANNON BLAZE AWAY by Joseph P. Thompson
THE STILL HOUR: *Communion with God in Prayer* by Austin Phelps
COLLECTED WORKS of James Henley Thornwell (4 vols.)
CALVINISM IN HISTORY *by Nathaniel S. McFetridge*
OPENING SCRIPTURE: *Hermeneutical Manual by Patrick Fairbairn*
THE ASSURANCE OF FAITH *by Louis Berkhof*
THE PASTOR IN THE SICK ROOM *by John D. Wells*
THE BUNYAN OF BROOKLYN: *Life & Sermons of I.S. Spencer*
THE NATIONAL PREACHER: *Sermons from 2nd Great Awakening*
FIRST THINGS: *First Lessons God Taught Mankind Gardiner Spring*
BIBLICAL & THEOLOGICAL STUDIES *by 1912 Faculty of Princeton*
THE POWER OF GOD UNTO SALVATION *by B.B. Warfield*
THE LORD OF GLORY *by B.B. Warfield*
A GENTLEMAN & A SCHOLAR: *Memoir of J.P. Boyce by J. Broadus*
SERMONS TO THE NATURAL MAN *by W.G.T. Shedd*
SERMONS TO THE SPIRITUAL MAN *by W.G.T. Shedd*
HOMILETICS AND PASTORAL THEOLOGY *by W.G.T. Shedd*
A PASTOR'S SKETCHES 1 & 2 *by Ichabod S. Spencer*
THE PREACHER AND HIS MODELS *by James Stalker*
IMAGO CHRISTI: *The Example of Jesus Christ by James Stalker*
LECTURES ON THE HISTORY OF PREACHING *by J. A. Broadus*
THE SHORTER CATECHISM ILLUSTRATED *by John Whitecross*
THE CHURCH MEMBER'S GUIDE *by John Angell James*
THE SUNDAY SCHOOL TEACHER'S GUIDE *by John A. James*
CHRIST IN SONG: *Hymns of Immanuel from All Ages by Philip Schaff*
COME YE APART: *Daily Words from the Four Gospels by J.R. Miller*
DEVOTIONAL LIFE OF THE S.S. TEACHER *by J.R. Miller*

Call us Toll Free at 1-877-666-9469
Send us an e-mail at sgcb@charter.net
Visit us on line at solid-ground-books.com
Uncovering Buried Treasure to the Glory of God

www.ingramcontent.com/pod-product-compliance
Lightning Source LLC
Chambersburg PA
CBHW051840040426
42447CB00006B/629